The *Characteristics* of a GOD MAN

TO: VERA
MAY THE PAGES OF THIS BOOK
BE A BLESSING TO YOU AND
YOUR FAMILY.
Bobby Thomas

The *Characteristics* of a GOD MAN

BOBBY THOMAS

ISBN: 978-1-947491-54-0
The Characteristics of a God man
Copyright © 2013 by Bobby S. Thomas

All rights reserved.

No part of this publication may be reproduced, distributed, or transmitted in any form or by any means, including photocopying, recording, or other electronic or mechanical methods, without the prior written permission of the publisher, except in the case of brief quotations embodied in critical reviews and certain other noncommercial uses permitted by copyright law.

Scripture quotations marked (KJV) are taken from the *Holy Bible, King James Version,* Cambridge, 1769. Used by permission. All rights reserved.

For permission requests, write to the publisher at the address below.

Yorkshire Publishing
3207 South Norwood Avenue
Tulsa, Oklahoma 74135
www.YorkshirePublishing.com
918.394.2665

Table of Contents

Foreword -- 7
Introduction -- 9

PART 1
The Process of Developing Spiritual Character ------- 13
Chapter 1 The Beast and the Lamb ------------------ 15
Chapter 2 Foundational Attitudes ------------------- 21
    The Poor in Spirit ----------------------------- 21
    The Mourners ---------------------------------- 24
    The Meek -------------------------------------- 28
Chapter 3 Developmental Attitudes ----------------- 31
    The Hungry and Thirsty ------------------------ 31
    The Merciful ---------------------------------- 36
    The Pure in Heart ----------------------------- 39
Chapter 4 Attitudes of Maturity -------------------- 43
    The Peacemakers ------------------------------- 43
    Persecuted for Righteousness's Sake ------------ 46
    The Reviled, Persecuted, and Evilly and Falsely Spoken of for Christ's Sake ------------------- 51
    Tests, Trials, and Tribulations ---------------- 53

PART 2
The Characteristics of a Godly Man ------------------ 57
Chapter 5 Characteristics of Christ ---------------- 59
Chapter 6 Ephesus, the Virgin ---------------------- 65
    Control -- 65
    Presence --------------------------------------- 85

Chapter 7 Smyrna Destitute ----------------------- 89
   Strength of Character ---------------------------- 89
Chapter 8 Pergamos Compromised ----------------- 95
   Decisiveness ------------------------------------- 95
Chapter 9 Thyatira, the Influenced Mother ---------- 101
   Jealous -- 101
Chapter 10 Sardis Prostitute / Drug Addict --------- 115
   Insight and Control ----------------------------- 115
Chapter 11 Philadelphia Recovered Drug Addict ----- 125
   Clean, Real, and Wealthy ------------------------ 125
Chapter 12 Laodicea Self-Sufficient
Business Woman ------------------------------- 141
   Final Authority --------------------------------- 141
Chapter 13 Transparency --------------------------- 152
   Fitting the Pattern ------------------------------ 155

Conclusion -------------------------------------- 161

Foreword

The author, Pastor Bobby Thomas, Sr. started his faith walk with the Lord at the age of 16. During his formative years, he was very active in his church and has continued to be faithful throughout his life. He developed a love for the Word of God and became an avid reader of the Bible. He acknowledged his call to the ministry at the age of 19 and began ministering without a pulpit. Through the divine leading of God, he also developed a quest to address his personal spiritual character. This dynamic is, all too often, missing from Christendom. As an outgrowth of both his call to ministry and his living a life of integrity, God has continued to bless him.

He is a successful husband, father, pastor, and businessman. He is the father of 3 sons and 1 daughter. In the year 2000, he established, the Church of God in Christ of Charleston located in Charleston, West Virginia. Pastor Thomas is Superintendent of the Northern District, state trustee board member, and chief adjutant for the Greater West Virginia Jurisdiction of the Church of God in Christ. Pastor Thomas is also an author and owner of Thomas Construction Company.

I count it a privilege to be asked to write the foreword for this book. It is fundamentally biblical, doctrinally sound and is a prophetic word that comes at a pivotal time in contemporary church history. We know that God has given power to the church. The question is, through what delivery method has God chosen to demonstrate this power? I believe God has chosen spirit-filled believers with personal spiritual character.

I strongly recommend that the people of God purchase and read this on-time, end-time, divine leading book.

—Bishop Henderson Wheeler, Sr.
Church of God in Christ, Inc.
Greater West Virginia Jurisdiction

Introduction

The US census report shows that approximately 30 percent of all children born today are born out of wedlock. That is an alarming statistic; but in the black community, it is an epidemic, reaching close to 70 percent. I believe that God has ordained the family to be the basic building block of society. What is happening in today's family is no accident. It is a calculated plan from Satan to overthrow God and be like the Most High.

As you may very well know, Lucifer was the guardian of the earth in the first creation. He was lifted up in pride by the very power that had been given by God (Isaiah 14:14, KJV). His goal was and is to be like God, for which he was cast down. As a result, Adam or mankind was set as guardian of the earth in his stead. Having lost his glory as Lucifer, Satan needs two things to accomplish his goal. Number one, he needs to assume his position as guardian of the earth, and number two, he needs to raise an army to overthrow God.

He needed guardianship of the earth to have a legal place of operation and to expand his forces. Revelation 12:8 (KJV) states that the dragon, which is Satan, drew the third part of the stars of God. In order to fight against God, he had to raise an army to equal the forces in heaven. God had two-thirds of his sons, and one-third went with Satan. The expansion of Satan's forces came through fallen humanity. In Satan's mind, his one-third forces of the sons of God and the expansion through fallen humanity would be enough to fight in the battle of Armageddon and overthrow God (Revelation 16).

As we all know, the return of the Lord is closer than ever, and Satan has escalated his plan to expand his armies. The family is the image of God on earth. Satan has to destroy this image to be like God. In respect to the creation of man, we can view God in a twofold manner: One, a life giver—he breathed the breath of life into Adam, and he became a living soul (Genesis 2:7, KJV). Two, a provider—he gave man everything he needed to be sustained in this earth (Genesis 2, KJV). Mathematically, it can be viewed as life giver plus provider equals to God.

One of the reasons Satan is so adamant against the family is that it is a direct reflection of God. After the fall, Adam named his wife Eve, which means mother of all living or life giver. God told Adam he would have to work by the sweat of his brow, which meant that he was a provider. In Genesis 3, Adam, the provider, and Eve, the life giver, sets the image of God in humanity. Even in their fallen state, they are God's image through marriage. Marriage in the sight of God is a constant rebuke to Satan that he can never be the Most High. Marriage means one man and one woman. But it is the plan of Satan to distort and destroy the family. I also think that so many children are being born out of wedlock to escalate Satan's plan to build an army. With our society suffering from the lack of discipline that comes from manhood, unruly children are poised to be taken by Satan at will. As the return of the Lord approaches,

Satan's time is limited. There is a calculated plan to condition men to enlist in Satan's army.

For instance, how in the world could a whole culture be influenced by prison practices? Sagging pants, baggy clothes, and violent speech are a few examples. It's bad enough that the black culture has swallowed these hook, line, and sinker, but other cultures around the world are also being affected by this poison. Where are the godly men that are standing in the gap to provide the alternative to this poison? In many cases, they have also been influenced.

Romans 8:22–23 (KJV) says, "For we know that the whole creation groaneth and travaileth in pain together until now. And not only they, but ourselves also, which have the first fruits of the Spirit, groan within ourselves, waiting for the adoption, to wit, the redemption of our body." With men being controlled by the will of Satan at large, there is a deep gnawing in the belly of womanhood and childhood for the appearance of the sons of God in this earth. The earth itself has been misused so badly; it also groans for the adoption of the sons of God and to witness the day when their natural bodies will be transformed into spiritual bodies to have dominion over the earth. There is famine in our world for godly men.

During the Creation, I believe the earth was poised to have righteous men care and wisely use her resources. Instead, she has been filled with the blood of men that came through unrighteousness. We are living in a sick world, and the earth itself is groaning to see when the bodies of godly men will be united to their spirits to carry out the will of God upon her surface.

With society moving at a fast pace away from the things of God, something has to be done. It is easy to say the earth is on an evitable course of destruction and simply ride it out. But as Christians, we have the responsibility to slow down the pace and enable as many people as possible to enter the kingdom of God. How do we slow the hands of time and move back to God's original purpose? One thing that could be done is backtrack to find out how we've gotten off track. But to get back will be no simple task. There is neither a single nor a simple answer. But I believe that part of the solution lies in the making of godly men.

In God's plan for humanity, redemption was pre-arranged. The answer came in an individual that was God enough to pick up a laid-down life, and man enough to shed blood to appease the wrath of God. This individual was known as the Son of God, Son of Man, or Jesus Christ. He is the original God-man and the pattern for all men. In this book, I will be releasing God-given revelations concerning the original God-man, Jesus Christ, and the patterns he has left for all men. This book is in two parts. Part one deals with personal development from spiritual infancy to spiritual maturity. Part two deals with the interaction of godly manhood with womanhood.

PART 1

The Process of Developing Spiritual Character

The Beast and the Lamb

Jesus is the Son of God, conceived of the Holy Ghost and the only begotten Son of God the Father. He is the Son of Man born of the Virgin Mary and has walked this earth the same as you and I. From his birth to the time of his public ministry, he had to have noticed the depraved condition of humankind. By the age of twelve, he understood his purpose for being here. After an incident upon traveling, he replied to Joseph and Mary, "Wist ye not that I must be about my father's business?" (Luke 2:49, KJV).

Jesus and his disciples had also been invited to a marriage feast in Cana of Galilee. Having a purpose in hand and seeing the conditions of the world, it would seem that he would be somewhat anxious to answer the cry of man's depravation. Yet, that was not the case at all. Perhaps the Son of God had seen final destiny and was reluctant to speed it along. Or could it be that the Son of Man had come to enjoy the works of his own hands at this feast? Maybe it wasn't so bad living in this world after all. Somehow, his mother, Mary, had some understanding as to the abilities that were resident within the Son of Man. She was the one who had become somewhat anxious to put on display the abilities of God. They were at the marriage feast and had run out of wine. Mary approached Jesus with a simple statement: "They have no wine." She did not ask him if he could make wine. She already knew that he could. Maybe in her own motherly way, she was trying to push him toward destiny. Jesus replied to her, "Woman, what have I to do with thee? Mine hour is not yet come" (John 2:4, KJV).

The only people that saw the power of God at work were those that bought the water pots. Now the cat was out of the bag, and Jesus was thrust into public ministry. Every great leader has a following. With Jesus, it was first his mother, then the pot carriers, and he would handpick certain brethren to follow him. The works of God pulled the brethren in as disciples and drew a multitude of people (Matthew 4:24–25, KJV)

It was here that the thoughts he had pondered were to be revealed. It was now his time. Matthew 5:1–2 (KJV) says, "And seeing the multitudes, he went up into a mountain: and when he was set, his disciples came unto him: And he opened his mouth and taught them." In other words, he saw the condition of humanity. Having perfect understanding of his Father's predestined plan, he saw how far humanity had digressed from where God intended for them to be. There was an urgency to speak. Thus, he opened his mouth and taught them. What was getting ready to come out of his mouth was the chalk line for spiritual growth. He was revealing to mankind God's will for spiritual growth.

There are two mentalities at work in the earth. The first is that of the beast. We see this in the seventh chapter of the book of Daniel, the prophet. There were four beasts that arose out of the sea. These four beasts represent four kingdoms. The first was like a lion and had eagle's wings. The second was like a bear with three ribs in its mouth. The third was like a leopard with four wings like a fowl and four heads. The fourth beast did not have a similitude, only that it was dreadful, terrible, and exceedingly strong. It also had teeth of iron and ten horns. These represented the kingdoms of the earth. In Matthew chapter four Jesus is lead by the Spirit into the wilderness to fast for forty days. During this time, Satan took him to an exceeding high place and showed him the kingdoms of the world. He offered the kingdoms to Jesus if he would bow down and worship him. Therefore, the kingdoms of the world are under the influence of Satan. Within these kingdoms, Satan uses the tactic of divide and conquer. The succeeding kingdom conquered the former. This is what I call the beast mentality. It uses brute force along with the wealth of the world to conquer and get ahead. This mentality was birthed out of the bowels of Satan. The second of the two mentalities is that of a Lamb. Jesus was about to reveal the nature of the Lamb by opening his mouth.

The flavor of all humanity, including the religious world, is that of the beast. We can see this by certain Jewish sects that had arisen and strove against one another. The works of the devil had permeated every sector of society. The first book of John 3:8 (kjv) lets us know that Jesus was manifest to destroy the works of the devil. It was in this setting and the conversations in the synagogues that seared the knowledge of God in the heart of Jesus. It was the knowledge that Satan was in control in this earth.

Jesus's mission was far higher than that of earthly kingdoms. Therefore, he did not build an army to overthrow the present regime. He was about to build a kingdom that was everlasting and not built with the works of man. In order to become part of this kingdom, one would have to be delivered from the beast mentality. The earth was about to experience something it had never seen from its conception. God had hinted at it by giving the law, but spiritually destitute hearts could not perceive nor grasp God's way from the law. Now the world was about to be influenced with the mentality of the Lamb.

When Jesus was set and his disciples came to him, he began to expound to them the way of the Lamb. He understood the bondages where Satan held them through the beast mentality. But they would learn how to be freewill prisoners of Christ, performing the will of God through the mentality of the Lamb.

Being a builder, I understand the components of a solid structure. You must have a foundation, a frame, and finish. The foundation is the support system for the building. The frame gives the building its skeletal structure and basic appearance. And the finish, cosmetically and uniformly, brings the building to its final appearance.

What was ready to come out of Jesus's mouth is commonly called the be-attitudes. It was also referred to as be-attitudes, or attitudes one should have. Since we are all too familiar with the mind of the beast, let's explore the mind of the Lamb. In doing so, we will look at three aspects of spiritual development, which correspond to the components of a solid building structure.

There are nine be-attitudes or aspects broken down into three sets of three.

The first three aspects give a foundation for spiritual development called foundational attitudes. The second three aspects give frame and structure called developmental attitudes. Finally, the last three aspects, which give a finish, are called the attitudes of maturity.

Lesson 1
- The beast mentality – Divide and conquer
- The Lamb mentality – Meek and humble
- Foundational attitudes
- Developmental attitudes
- Attitudes of maturity

Foundational Attitudes

The Poor in Spirit

The first thing that Jesus said was "Blessed is the poor in spirit: for theirs is the kingdom of heaven." To be blessed is to be happy. The poor are those that are destitute and, for some reason, cannot help themselves. The spirit is the part of man that comes from God, the vehicle that intrinsically ties us to God.

There are two types of people that are poor in spirit. There are those that are not aware of it, or they may be aware but powerless to do anything about it. Then there are the blessed poor in spirit. These people have come to understand the degenerative nature of man. They understand a fig-leafed Adam, who had been stripped of the glory and presence of God. The fig leaf was an artificial covering that they hid behind (Genesis 3:21–24, KJV). The blessed poor in spirit are those that understand as David did in Psalms 51:5 (KJV): "Behold, I was shapen in iniquity; and in sin did my mother conceive me." They have come to understand that they are broken and cut off from the source who made them. They are in need of repair.

To be the blessed poor in spirit is to understand that we are cut off from God and have the nature of the beast. This nature has to be broken. The process of breaking the nature of the beast is called contrition. Isaiah 66:1–3 (KJV) says,

> Thus saith the Lord, The heaven is my throne, and the earth is my footstool: where is the house that ye build unto me? And where is the place of my rest? For all those things hath mine hand made, and all those things have been, saith the Lord: but to this man will I look, even to him that is poor and of a contrite spirit, and trembleth at my word. He that killeth an ox is as if he slew a man; he that sacrificeth a lamb, as if he cut off a dog's neck; he that offereth an oblation, as if he offered swine's blood; he that burneth incense, as if he blessed an idol. Yea, they have chosen their own ways, and their soul delighteth in their abominations.

God, showing his greatness, says the heaven is his throne and the earth is his footstool. Where is his place of rest? What could be an appropriate place of God's dwelling with men? King David, at man's best attempt, built a temple for him to dwell through his son Solomon. But God's pleasure was not in that kind of building but in a building that is poor and of a contrite spirit, trembling at the word of God. Such a building is the heart of man that has been changed to the point that to slay an ox is the same as slaying a man or sacrificing a lamb is the same as severing the neck of man's trusted friend, the dog.

The blessed poor in spirit have a need for revival of spirit; they need to be tapped into the source from which they came. They need God. Isaiah 57:15 (KJV) says,

> For thus saith the high and lofty One that inhabiteth eternity, whose name is Holy; I dwell in the high and holy place, with him also that is of a contrite and humble spirit, to revive the spirit of the humble, and to revive the heart of the contrite ones.

In other words, these are the people that can dwell with God—the one that is humble, having broken the beast spirit. They have a reviving and reuniting of spirit to God.

There is a distinct blessing that comes from being the blessed poor in spirit: theirs is the kingdom of heaven. That means the entrance to the kingdom of heaven is to be the blessed poor in spirit. This is the entrance key to the mind-set of the Lamb or the kingdom of heaven. When you become broken, you are at the door to the kingdom of heaven. Psalms 34:18 (kjv) says, "The Lord is nigh unto them that are of a broken heart; and saveth such as be of a contrite spirit." This attitude opens the entrance to the kingdom of heaven. The blessed poor in spirit correspond to the building process as the most stable soil and only basis for true Christian development. It is the foundation and support for true Christianity.

The Mourners

"Blessed are they that mourn: for they shall be comforted." Mourning happens when there has been a great loss, such as the demise of a loved one. Though one is loved dearly, the realization of not coming back is evident. This is mourning for total loss. Once we have entered the door to the kingdom of heaven through Jesus, there is mourning that goes on in our soul and spirit. There is a mourning of soul because the natural or fleshly man has come to love the delicacies that the beastly nature has provided. A good example would be Israel being delivered from Egypt. It was a spiritual thing for God to deliver them, with such a great deliverance and without military force. But after they were out of Egypt and had faced adversity, their flesh or human nature began to cry out for what it had once known (Exodus 16:3, kjv). Therefore, there was a longing for what they could not have. The part of them that was cut off was still available, but they could not have it and deliverance at the same time. Their souls mourned for the fleshpots of Egypt, which was a provision of the beast or bread of bondage. It is the process of mourning that teaches us to have a new diet. God was teaching them to eat the bread of freedom. They had been sustained by Egypt or the beast for 430 years. They then had to learn how to be sustained by God.

As creations of God, we might be referred to as living intelligence. We are recorders, and everything that passes our way is forever recorded. In actuality, all the information that has ever been before us is available to us. Your flesh never forgets what it has been in contact with. For a follower of Christ, that is a source of mourning. Even though we are recorders, spiritually we are broken. We do not have perfect recall of all the information that has come before us. Our spiritual recordings are vague, but our fleshly recordings are vivid. Therefore, fleshly encounters are prevalent to our memories. Satan makes sure of it. This is why Jesus says the Holy Ghost will bring all things to our remembrance. All the things spoken of by Jesus are spiritual things in which Satan has no interest. The things he had revealed to the disciples would invoke the Holy Spirit to bring them back, not only bring to remembrance, but also reveal things to come (John 14:26, 16:13, kjv).

There is also mourning in the spirit for total loss. This mourning happens once you come into the kingdom of heaven and your eyes are opened to the destitutions you have lived in. There is mourning because of hopelessness and despair. Satan has literally robbed you. The fleshly part of you is maimed for the rest of your natural life. The spirit man has to drag the carnal man to where he needs to be. When the spirit man is finally alive or in tune with God, we can finally see that we have been stripped of education, intelligence, health, strength, dignity, and more importantly, the peace and joy of God. Some things can be regained, but others are totally lost. You can see where you are and where you should be and also what you have and what you should have. Your spirit feels the loss. This causes mourning in the spirit.

Thank God for his mercy and grace, for Jesus said that the mourners would be comforted. One is comforted when drawn near, for example, a child being held in the bosom of his mother or father. Comfort comes as a result of justice in that a murderer is brought to justice. Therefore, one finds resolve and closure in justice. Comfort comes through forgiveness. One realizes the loss can never be regained and comes to resolution and closure through forgiveness. Comfort also comes when one receives direction. When we are at a loss, many times, we don't know which way to go. When direction comes, we find comfort in direction. Jesus found comfort in direction. For the joy that was set before him, he endured the cross Hebrews 12:2, kjv. Similarly, believers receive comfort in knowing their destination. Paul wrote to the Thessalonians saying, comfort ye one another with these words. When we get a sense of direction as to where we are going from the point of loss, we find comfort. We shall be caught up to meet him in the clouds and be with the Lord forever (1 Thessalonians 4:13–18, kjv).

The ultimate form of comfort for the spiritual man are the words Jesus spoke in John 14. He said he was going away but would not leave him comfortless. The job of comfort was performed by the Son of God when he was physically present on earth. His ability to change whatever situation was a comfort to the disciples and those that came in contact with him. There was a sense of distress in his acknowledgement that he was going away. Peter said, "Where shall we go? Only you have the words to eternal life." Jesus said, "I will not leave you comfortless. I will send you another Comforter, which is the Holy Ghost. He is the spirit of truth and will lead and guide you into all truth." At this point in spiritual development, the indwelling of the Holy Spirit is vitally important. He is the one that empowers the believer to continue on the Christian walk. He awakens new desires for righteousness, prayer, fasting, and seeking the face of God. He is the one that ultimately empowers the spiritual man to be a witness for Christ in the midst of adversity and the perverted world.

In Mark 10:23–30 (KJV), after Jesus finished speaking about how much harder it is for a rich man to enter into heaven than for a camel to go through the eye of a needle, Peter got very concerned. He was floored in the fact that they had given up everything to follow Jesus, and from the words of Jesus, they wouldn't be able to make it in. Peter had suffered great loss to follow Christ, and for what? Jesus comforted them with his words that they would be blessed one hundredfold in this world and that in the world to come, they would have eternal life. In the building process a firm foundation consists of excavated earth to the shape of the building, concrete footings reinforced with steel bars and masonry blocks. The first stage gave us the most stable soil. Mourning represent adding reinforced concrete to the firmest soil in the building of the spiritual man.

The Meek

"Blessed are the meek: for they shall inherit the earth." I want to look at meekness in two ways. First, in common understanding and secondly, in what God has revealed to me. In common understanding, meekness is to be humble and have strength under control. Meekness is not weakness but power under control. Jesus exercised this trait in the Crucifixion experience. When the soldiers came with Judas Iscariot to apprehend Jesus, Peter drew his sword and cut the ear of one of the soldiers. Jesus rebuked him because Peter was trying to fight a spiritual battle in a physical way. Jesus put the soldier's ear back on and submitted to the capture. The fact that he submitted was not that he was weak, but meek. He had enough power at his disposal to wipe out the entire Roman empire. He could have called ten thousand angels to do his bidding. One angel can put a thousand men to flight, and two can put ten thousand to flight. Well, what if he called ten thousand? He was powerful with meekness. He had power under control.

The second way I would like to look at meekness is in accordance with the text and the pattern of spiritual development. Here it means to relinquish the right to reclaim the past or fight for the future. The idea is that you are in Christ and the Lord now orders your steps.

The nature of the beast is to devour, divide, and conquer. So is the mentality of the world. In order to get ahead, you have to fight, step on others, and destroy whatever or whomever gets in your way. Does this sound familiar to you? Yes, it is the nature of the beast, the attitude that is broken by the nature of the Lamb.

When Jesus was here on earth physically, the beastly nature did as it had always done and devoured the Lamb of God through the Crucifixion. In doing so, the nature of the Lamb assumed its position not only on earth but also in heaven. By humbling himself, Jesus gave up the right to fight. This action correctly places him in authorship of meekness.

Numbers 12:1–16 (KJV) speaks of the meekness of Moses. Miriam and Aaron spoke against Moses because he had married an Ethiopian woman. Moses did not fight them over the issue. God came to Moses's rescue suddenly. The idea here is that God fights for those who have developed spiritual meekness in the kingdom of heaven. God fought Moses's battle because he had relinquished the right to fight. It was not that Moses was not able to fight for himself. He had learned to let God do the fighting when he has sent him. When Moses first understood his mission, he took it upon himself to rescue one of his brethren who was being mistreated. In this case, he killed an Egyptian. So you see, Moses was very well able to take care of himself. His experience with God made him meek. He was a very strong man capable of committing murder, but his strength was now controlled by meekness.

The Bible lets us know that God beautifies the meek with salvation (Psalms 194:4, KJV). That means they will receive eternal life and the joy of seeing God fight their battles and making them victorious in every battle.

In order to obtain this benefit, one must have put on meekness as a way of life. God will not fight for those with a facade of meekness. One must obtain a state of meekness for God to come to their rescue in this way. The beastly nature makes us want to fight. This is a deterrent to God helping us. When we fight, we take matters into our own hands, thus tying the hands of God.

The promise to the meek is that they will inherit the earth. If we look at the world that we live in, it is a fight to obtain wealth, land, status, position, and prestige. What the nature of the beast caused you to fight and struggle for, the meek will inherit. Meekness is the part of the foundational attitudes that adds concrete masonry blocks to the footings, completing the strongest spiritual foundation possible.

Lesson 2–Summary of Foundational Attitudes

- The poor in spirit – the awareness that you are broken and separated from God
- Entrance to kingdom of heaven
- The mourners–experiencing total loss by giving up everything to follow Jesus Christ
- Comfort by being filled with the Holy Ghost
- The meek – power under control, giving up the right to fight for the future or reclaim the past
- Inheriting by performing kingdom work

Developmental Attitudes

The Hungry and Thirsty

"Blessed are they which do hunger and thirst after righteousness: for they shall be filled" (Matthew 5:6 KJV). Hunger is the discomfort, pain, or weakness caused by the need for food. Thirst is the uncomfortable or distressful feeling caused by the desire or need for water.

To deal with this stage of spiritual development, we must talk about the seat of hunger and thirst. Man consists of three parts: body, soul, and spirit. The body, or flesh, is called the carnal man. The Greek word and pronunciation is *sarkikos* (sar-kee-kos'). It is the seat of animal cravings as to eat and drink. The soul is called the natural man. The Greek word and pronunciation is *psuchikos* (psoo-khee-kos). It is the animate part of man and the seat of the affections and emotions. The spirit of man is called the spiritual man. The Greek word and pronunciation is *pneumatikos* (pnyoo-mat-ik-os'). It is non-carnal and supernatural. It is the seat of the will and intellect. It is also the seat of spiritual desire as in worshipping God and the desire for righteousness, holiness, joy, and peace.

The soul is intricately united to the body, and the spirit to the soul. The flesh is what puts us in contact with this physical world and its surroundings. The man's soul, with an unregenerate spirit, will be filled with the delicacies of this world. Part of Satan's seat is in the flesh of man. It is through this part of man that the will of Satan is carried out. In John 8:44 (KJV), Jesus speaks to the scribes and Pharisees, saying, "Ye are of your father the Devil and the lusts of your father will ye do." This indicates Satan's link to the flesh. Without the spirit of man being revived through the work of Christ, the soul man is basically powerless against the cravings of the flesh.

Thus we can see the importance of the foundational attitudes, which shows brokenness, total loss, and giving up the right to fight. It is at this point that the spiritual man has the proper foundation for true spiritual development. Without the foundational attitudes, one will tend to reject spiritual principles. 1 Corinthians 2:14 (KJV) says, "But the natural man receives not the things of the Spirit of God: for they are foolishness unto him: neither can he know them, because they are spiritually discerned."

It is imperative that we have a strong foundation of brokenness through repentance. We have to count gain in the flesh as total loss, then relinquish the right to regain that which has been lost or struggle to gain what is in the future. If we pick up the things we left behind, we make ourselves transgressors. Paul said, "For if I build again the things I destroyed, I make myself a transgressor" (Galatians 2:18 KJV). If I fight to claim the future, then I have reverted to the old nature and make myself subject to the nature of the beast. This is the attitude that puts us in the place to have God fight for us. This is a difficult principle, and I am sure there will be a lot of discussion and concern over it. If we truly submit, God will move on our behalf in ways we have never known.

There are two seats of hunger in man. One is for the carnal man. To him, hunger and thirst is the craving for food and water, which are normal. This seat is tied into the basic works of the flesh. The food and water taken in become the fuel for unrighteous living. It gives a place for the works of the flesh to thrive. In the unregenerate state, nourishment to the body drives the beastly nature and holds us captive even against our own will.

The second seat of hunger is in the spirit. If you could look at people in the spirit, you would see a picture of malnourished spirits. They have skinny legs and big bellies, and tears come out of their eyes for lack of proper nourishment. It is the carnal man's job to keep it this way. To our flesh, the answer to hunger is food. The answer to thirst is water. To the spirit man, the answer to hunger is the word of God. In Matthew 4, Jesus fasted for forty days. Afterward, he was hungry. Fasting quiets the cravings of the flesh, which can be equated in some respects to the voice of Satan. Satan came to test him at his weakest point. If the spirit man had not been nurtured, maybe he would have turned a stone into bread to fuel the flesh, thus giving Satan rule in his life. Instead, his reply to Satan was that man should not live by bread alone, but by every word that proceeds out of the mouth of God. He was letting us know that there is another side of man that needs to be nourished, the spirit man. He was also letting us know that the spirit man is to be fed by the word of God. As long as one does not receive the work of Christ on the cross, the spirit man is powerless to help himself. The spirit man is still powerless and bound to follow the nature of the beast. The First Epistle of Peter 2:1–2 (kjv) lets us know that we should desire the sincere milk of the word as newborn babes. There again the word of God is milk to the new convert and food to the mature. The basis of receiving the sincere milk is to break the nature of the beast by laying aside all malice, guile, hypocrisies, envying, and evil speaking.

John 1:1 (kjv) says, "In the beginning was the Word, the Word was with God, and the Word was God." Verse 14 in the same chapter says, "And the Word was made flesh, and dwelt among us (and we beheld his glory, the glory as of the only begotten of the Father) full of grace and truth." These two verses let us know that Jesus is the Word of God. He alone is the one that satisfies the cravings for hunger in the spirit. In John 6:35 (kjv), Jesus said, "I am the bread of life: he that cometh to me shall never hunger." Here again, he is the source of food for the spirit man. In order to have spiritual nourishment, we must come to him.

The cravings of the spirit man are to worship God, to take in his word, to be righteous, and to have joy and peace. Without the foundational attitudes, the cravings of the spirit man will never be released.

There are also two seats of thirst in man. The answer to thirst in the flesh is water. The answer of thirst for the spirit man is the Holy Spirit. In John 4,

Jesus met a Samaritan woman at one of Jacob's wells. He said that he would give her water where she would never thirst again. Such is the well of waters springing up in everlasting life. The water and thirsting that he was talking about couldn't have been that of natural means since they were at a viable well, and she had the means to draw the water. He was speaking of a thirst in the spirit man.

In John 7:37–39 (KJV), Jesus said, "If any man thirst let him come unto me and drink. He that believeth on me as the scripture hath said shall flow out of his belly rivers of living water. But this spoke he of the Spirit, which they that believe on him should receive." So we see the Holy Spirit is spiritual water.

There is a promise to those that do hunger and thirst after righteousness that they will be filled. Righteousness is fulfilled in two ways. One is an imputation of righteousness. We are proclaimed righteous through the shed blood of Jesus Christ when we believe in him (Phil. 3:9, kjv). Second is the growth process of righteousness. It comes through the word of God and the Holy Ghost. We hunger and thirst for righteousness. The word of God fulfills hunger for righteousness, and the Holy Ghost fulfills thirsting for righteousness.

The process of being declared righteous and growing in righteousness weeds out the beast mentality. It then weaves in the nature of the Lamb.

In this part of the building process the deck or floor is laid which represent hungering and thirsting after righteousness.

The Merciful

"Blessed are the merciful: for they shall obtain mercy." To be merciful is to be full of mercy, showing compassion and having pity. Mercy is a divine benefit. It encompasses forgiveness and divine grace. It is the ability to look beyond one's present state of being to see God's purpose for them. In God's eyes, everyone is salvageable. Mercy gives others the possibility of salvation. The First Epistle of Peter 3:9 (KJV) says, "The Lord is not slack concerning his promise, as some men count slackness; but is longsuffering to us-ward, not willing that any should perish, but that all should come to repentance." Regardless of the past, it is the will of God that all people have the opportunity for salvation.

Luke 23 gives an account of Jesus's Crucifixion. While being taunted by the onlookers, he said, "Father, forgive them for they know not what they do." Thank God for the nature of the Lamb that humbled himself to the death of the cross. If he had the nature of the beast, all those that were involved, including innocent people, would have been destroyed. Furthermore, all men would not have the opportunity for salvation. What Jesus did when he said, "Father forgive them" was to exemplify the epitome of mercy. He afforded those who crucified him the privilege of salvation. This is the nature of the Lamb at best.

Considering where God has brought each of us from, there is no deed that can be done that extends past the mercy of God. That is except blasphemy of the Holy Ghost. We all deserve the penalty of death brought on us through Adam. God in his mercy gave tender lambs, which humbly submitted for the atoning of Israel's sin. But we have a better sacrifice, the Lamb of God, who has done the same for all humanity. He died for us while we were fighting against him. While we were yet sinners, he died showing God's mercy to humanity. For this cause, we are saved today.

Psalm 103 lets us know that God is merciful. Mercy is a part of his character. He is slow to anger and plenteous in mercy. He also remembers that we are but dust. He has pity on us as a father pities his children. His mercy is from everlasting to everlasting and endures forever.

In return for being merciful, mercy shall be obtained. There are at least two ways obtaining mercy can be looked at—receiving mercy and being in a spiritual state of mercy. Galatians 6 speaks of reaping and sowing. Whatever you sow you shall reap. So is the case with mercy. If you sow mercy, you shall reap mercy. It is certain that we all need mercy in our lives if no more than the penalty of Adam's sin. Also in times of failure, we need mercy. But I think what Paul was talking about extends beyond sowing and reaping. It gets into having the character of God. To obtain mercy is to start to be more like God. You begin to see as he sees and operate like he operates. You begin to have the heart of God toward all mankind. This type of mercy is what the spiritual person must get a hold on. It is not turn on / turn off in certain situations, but it is constant; even in the face of death. When spiritual persons have obtained mercy, they can face death by their peers and still allow them space to be saved. Such was the case of Stephen in Acts 7. After preaching the word of God, the religious people began to stone him. He had to have developed the spiritual characteristic of having obtained mercy. While he was being stoned, the heavens opened up. God came to see about the meek. As the heavens opened, it was God's way of saying to Stephen, "What do you want me to do?" Stephen replied out of mercy, exemplifying the nature of the Lamb. He said, "Lord lay not this sin to their charge." He could have said, "Lord save me," at which point the angels would have come and destroyed all that were involved, including spectators. But by doing otherwise, he displayed the development of obtaining mercy. He left his murderers the possibility of salvation.

There was a young man during this time who was consenting to the death of Stephen. His name was Saul. He continued on the course to destroy the church. Shortly afterward he met Jesus head on, he was converted and became the apostle to the Gentiles. If Stephen did not obtain mercy, Saul could have been condemned to hell. Today, you and I are afforded the privilege of holding the apostle Paul, a former murderer, and his writings in high esteem because Stephen obtained the mercy of God. If it had not been for the developmental stage of obtaining mercy, we may not have what we call the Pauline letters today.

Obtaining mercy adds to the spiritual house walls, the roof structure, windows and doors such that the form of the house can be clearly seen.

The Pure in Heart

"Blessed are the pure in heart: for they shall see God." The heart is the most central part of something. Proverbs 4:22 (KJV) says that the issues of life come out of it. Issues of life coming out of the heart have two meanings. First, in that the heart is a physical blood pump. Leviticus 17:10 (KJV) lets us know that the life of the flesh is in the blood. All nutrients the body needs flow through the bloodstream. Therefore, it can be called the center of operation for the carnal man. The issues of life flow from it.

Secondly, there is a heart of the spirit, which should not be confused with the physical blood pump. This was the heart that Jesus was speaking of when he said, "Blessed are the pure in heart." The spiritual heart is the center of operation for the spirit man. While within the fleshly heart are desires and cravings of the flesh, the spiritual heart craves the will of God. One day, the disciples noticed that Jesus hadn't eaten for a few days. As any concerned follower, they approached him to ask him to eat. Jesus replied that his meat was to do the will of the one that sent him (John 4:34, KJV). Even though the fleshly man needs nutrients to survive, the higher call of survival is the will of God. In this stage of development, we leave the importance of worldly success and focus on the purpose for which God designed us, that is to fulfill the will of God. The preceding foundations and levels of development bring us to the point where our focus will not be centered on the appetites of the flesh but on the will of God.

The core of your being, the base of your operation has been purified. If it were not so, the beastly nature would cause you to strive that you might live. Then you might do deceitful things of dishonesty to survive. When you are developed to be pure in heart, you have the right motives, which are given you through spiritual development. Your base of operation and existence depend on what God wants you to do. At this point, you will literally give your life for the cause of the kingdom of heaven.

It is this level of development that I call eternal security. Development at this point locks you in with God. This is why Paul, being set free through the blood of Jesus, could turn around and say, "I am a prisoner of the Lord Jesus Christ." He had gotten locked in to the will of God. The press was no longer to the things of the flesh but a press toward the high calling of God in Jesus Christ (Ephesians 3:1, Philippians 3:14, KJV)

The promise to the pure in heart is that they shall see God. I feel that this is one of the only places in scripture where Jesus definitely and specifically tells us that we shall see God. Before now it has been understood that no man can see God and live. Ex. 33:20 At this level of development, you will see yourself operating like God . You are pure at heart, which guarantees that you will see God.

There are a couple of questions asked in Psalms 24:3–4 (KJV). "Who shall ascend into the hill of the Lord? Or who shall stand in his holy place? He that hath clean hands, and a pure heart; who hath not lifted up his soul to vanity, nor sworn deceitfully." Here the psalmist was speaking of the high priest among the Levites, which ministered to the things of God. Moses ascended to the hill of the Lord, and Aaron stood in the holy place. They had to have clean hands and a pure heart without vanity and deceit. If those were the things that qualified Moses and Aaron to enter into God's presence , then, how much more is required to ascend to the holy hill and the holy place in heaven? The acceptance of Jesus Christ along with the development process brings the believer to the point where they can see God. They are clean. The pure in heart has a promise; they shall see God.

At this point, the foundation is set, and the framed walls and the roof are on the spiritual house. That which was in blueprint form has become apparent to the onlooker. The developmental stage of pure in heart add to the building structure all the inner workings such as plumbing, electric, and HVAC. The light bulbs are on, and everyone can see what the house looks like. The owner and friends have their own ideas of decoration. However, the decoration belongs exclusively to the owner. Since this spiritual house belongs to God, it is he who will make the final details. Let's see how he does it as we enter into the attitudes of maturity.

Lesson3–Summary of Developmental Attitudes

- Hunger and thirst after righteousness – appetite for spiritual things are opened
- Spiritual hunger filled by the Word of God

- Spiritual thirst filled by the Spirit of God
- Merciful – the state of mercifulness
- Allowing others the opportunity to be saved
- Pure in heart – pure motives
- The ability to see God

Attitudes of Maturity

The Peacemakers

"Blessed are the peacemakers: for they shall be called the children of God." Peacemaking is an attitude of spiritual maturity or a spiritual state of being. It looks through the present conditions and conflict to the end of peace. It should not be thought of as an act for resolving personal conflicts only. The higher end of peacemaking is to bring individuals to the righteousness of God through Jesus Christ—that is, to bring people to peace with God. Colossians 1:20 (KJV) says, "And, having made peace through the blood of his cross, by him to reconcile all things unto himself; by him, I say, whether they be things in earth, or things in heaven." Jesus is the vehicle that connected man to God in heaven. The two were reconciled through his blood, which appeased the wrath of God toward mankind—that is, to all that received the precious gift.

What we know of as peace in this world is contaminated through the sin of Adam. Isaiah 53:5 says, "He was wounded for our transgressions, he was bruised for our iniquities: the chastisement of our peace was upon him; and with his stripes we are healed." The chastisement or correction of our peace that was broken by Adam was upon Jesus Christ. In other words, we find peace with God through Jesus Christ. He gave us the correct peace. In John 14: 27 (kjv), Jesus said, "My peace I give unto you not as the world gives." He brought, to this world, true peace.

Peace is the fertile ground in which righteousness needs to grow. James 3:18 (kjv) says, "The fruit of righteousness is sown in peace of them that make peace." This is the peacemaker. He is the one that creates the atmosphere for righteousness to thrive. They hold open the door so that those that were in enmity against God might grow in righteousness. Peacemakers see the present condition of new converts but look toward their end in the will of God.

The new convert comes with all types of baggage. They must be allowed the opportunity to grow in righteousness. This is why Christians sometime seem hypocritical. They have not developed yet. With the eye of the peacemaker, they will be transformed by the will of God.

Hebrews 12:14 (kjv) says, "Follow peace with all men, and holiness, without which no man shall see the Lord." This verse mentions two things needed to see God, peace and holiness. Follow peace with all men, that is, to the end, it is God's will that all should come to repentance.

Peacemakers shall be called the children of God. What an honor and a privilege to be called a child of God. How do we know whose children we are? The Pharisees boasted on having Abraham as their father, which imperatively meant they were children of God. They had missed the whole picture of what Adam had done.

When Satan was expelled from heaven, he took one-third of the angels of God with him. In order to become like the Most High, he needed a way of expansion. His opportunity to expand was through the disobedience of Adam and Eve. He beguiled them to pledge their allegiance to him. By doing so, he became the father of all humanity. Jesus replied to the Pharisees, "You are of your father the devil and his deeds you will do" (John 8:44, KJV). Understanding, we are all born children of the devil, it is a blessing to reach the point where we are called God's children. Adam's sin aroused the wrath of God. Peacemakers pull people out of the wrath of God into righteousness and peace with God.

The first book of John 3:10 (KJV) says, "In this the children of God are manifest, and the children of the devil: whosoever doeth not righteousness is not of God, neither he that loveth not his brother." The defining lines between being children of God or children of the devil are the deeds that we do. If we follow the deeds of righteousness, we are the children of God. If we follow the deeds of the flesh, we are children of the devil (Colossians 3:4–6, KJV).

To be called the children of God, we have reached a level of maturity where we have been purged from dead works of the flesh through the blood of Jesus and the word of God, the blood of Jesus being the initiator and the word of God being the process of maturation (John 15:3, Heb. 9:14, KJV). Then we understand what it is to be called a child of God. It is to have reached a level of maturity where one's life is in obedience to the will of God.

At this level of the building process, the house is complete. Its details are out of the ordinary, yet very tasteful and pleasing to those who look upon it. All the other houses had open house such that everyone can see their interior detail. This house is different because the interior detail is only for the eye of its designer. Its external beauty along with it being a closed housed makes it a mystery to its community.

Persecuted for Righteousness's Sake

"Blessed are they which are persecuted for righteousness's sake: for theirs is the kingdom of heaven." To be persecuted is to be constantly harassed as to cause injury. At this level of maturity, righteousness has been obtained through the blood of Jesus and the growth process . At this point, the believer has become a threat to satanic institutions. Therefore, they are constantly pursued in order to stop the process of building the kingdom of heaven. In order for one to be persecuted for righteousness's sake, one must have obtained righteousness. It is evident that you cannot be persecuted for that which you do not have. Furthermore, it would be foolish to take persecution for that which is not in your possession. In Philippians 3 the apostle Paul says, "And be found in him, not having mine own righteousness, which is of the law, but that which is through the faith of Christ, the righteousness which is of God by faith." For this reason, Paul counted everything in his carnal life as a loss that he might gain Christ.

Persecution comes as a result of being out of the norm or ordinary. When the nature of the Lamb is developed in believers, it takes them out of the norms of this world. They become readily visible and vulnerable to attack because of the character of Christ that is in them. There is constant pressure from the nature of the beast to push spiritual people into his mold. This would render them ineffective to the kingdom of heaven. Paul says to the Romans, "Be not conformed to this world but be transformed by the renewing of your mind in Christ Jesus" (Rom. 12:2). Satan wants to keep people ordinary and in bondage to Adam's failure. God wants them to be extraordinary and free from Adam's failure such that they may live in Christ. God wants their lives to be a constant reminder to Satan that he is still in control.

Peter, being a follower of Christ, was still under the influence of the beastly nature. We see this when the soldiers came to pick up Jesus by betrayal through Judas's kiss. Peter took out his sword and cut off the ear of one of the soldiers. Jesus told Peter to put the sword up because he was not fighting that kind of battle. Peter assured and swore that he would go to the death with Jesus, but he lacked the spiritual maturity for such a task. Jesus, understanding the process of development, knew exactly where Peter stood. He replied, "You shall deny me three times before the cockcrow." In Matthew 26:69–75 (KJV), Peter could be spotted by the crowd because the process of spiritual growth had started in his life. He had already begun to resemble Jesus. A girl saw him and said he was with Jesus. Peter, lacking spiritual maturity, denied that he was with Jesus. Then another lady came to him, and he denied again. Then others came and told him that he even talked like Jesus. He cursed Jesus to save his neck. Peter had not reached the point where he could die for the sake of Christ. Matt. 26:69-74 As any immature follower of Christ would do, he reverted back to the beastly nature to get out of his life-threatening dilemma.

In Acts 12, we see a picture of a mature Peter. It is certain that his denying Jesus had crushed the will of Satan, that he would follow Jesus all the way. Herod killed James for preaching the gospel. People that lived in the norm of that time were pleased by such an action. Knowing for sure that Peter was a follower of Christ, they arrested him with intentions to kill him. At this point, he did not deny Jesus. He exemplified the nature of the Lamb and humbled himself to whatever would come. To be persecuted for righteousness's sake is a distinct mark of spiritual maturity.

Twice in the spiritual attitudes, Jesus promised the kingdom of heaven. The first time he mentioned it was in the foundational attitudes, "Blessed are the poor in spirit, for theirs is the kingdom of heaven." There, it is the key to the entrance of the kingdom of God. The second time this was mentioned was in the attitudes of maturity, "Blessed are they which are persecuted for righteousness's sake: for theirs is the kingdom of heaven." Here it means to take up residence. Being endowed with spiritual maturity makes residency in the kingdom of God. At this point, Jesus Christ captures the believer. Paul, in speaking to Philemon, said that he was a prisoner of Jesus Christ, indicating spiritual maturity and abode in the kingdom of heaven (Philemon 1:1, KJV). Jesus spoke to the church of Philadelphia in Revelation 3:12, saying he will make those that overcome pillars in the temple of God. Pillars are permanent supports in a building structure. Overcomers will be made permanent supports in the temple of God. Jesus could not have been talking about a physical temple of God. He was talking about a spiritual temple. This was the one that he raised up in three days. The place that God really wanted to dwell is in the hearts of men. The temple of God and the kingdom of heaven are synonymous. To be a pillar means that you are a permanent fixture. You can be trusted to carry the gospel to the death. For this, theirs is the kingdom of heaven.

I would like to add here that Jesus reconciled two ideologies in the beatitudes about eternal security. There is the Armenian view that basically says that one can be lost after being saved if they do not continue in the ways of Christ and the Calvinistic view that says all your sins are forgiven present, past, and future. Therefore, it doesn't matter what one does after being saved; their salvation is secure. The extreme of the Armenian view leads to legalism, and the extreme of Calvinism leads to lawlessness. The first beatitude shows entrance into the kingdom of heaven. Then there is a growth process. In the event of loss of life during the growth process, God is the judge. He is the only one who knows the intents of the hearts of men. The Bible says that marriage is honorable and the bed undefiled, but the adulterer and fornicator God will judge (Hebrews 13:4). With people being different and relationships so diverse, no man can look at any particular failed marriage and color it with a broad brush. According to the Bible, to marry again would be adultery. Even though the Bible says so, men do not have the authority to make the call because God will judge the adulterer and fornicator according to where they are. He has reserved this call for himself. As it is in this situation, I feel it is the same in the Christian growth process. God is the judge. He knows the thoughts and intents of the heart.

The eighth beattitude also promises the kingdom of heaven. After the growth process, which brings the believer to maturity, residency is established. The believer is willfully imprisoned by Christ. Entrance and residency reconcile the two seemingly opposing thoughts.

As stated, this spiritual house is a mystery and the authorities are processing and enforcing ordinances that cause it to stand outside the perimeters of the law. It is to the end of demolishing the structure. During this time the house becomes a safe place for those converted from the beast.

The Reviled, Persecuted, and Evilly and Falsely Spoken of for Christ's Sake

> Blessed are ye, when men shall revile you, and persecute you, and say all manner of evil against you falsely, for my sake. Rejoice, and be exceedingly glad: for great is your reward in heaven: for so persecuted they the prophets which were before you.
>
> St. Matthew 5:11 KJV

The beast, understanding that the believer will not move at simple persecution, begins to revile and make false accusations that will bring the believer to their demise. Once this type of persecution happens in the believer's life, they move to the highest level of maturity. It is only at this level of maturity that one can stand against the nature of the beast as a lamb.

At this point, the believer is a builder of the kingdom of heaven. The destruction of their lives will literally build the kingdom of heaven or temple of God. In John 2, Jesus, speaking to sign-seeking Jews, said that if they destroyed this temple, he would build it in three days. They thought of the forty years that it took to build the temple. Jesus was speaking of his death, which would create a new habitation for God through his people.

This level of maturity renders the believer helpless to fight against false accusations and reviling. In Matthew 27, as Jesus hung on the cross, an accusation was put above his head: This is Jesus, king of the Jews. The Jews mocked him, saying, "You saved others, save yourself." They reviled him, saying, "You said you would destroy the temple and build it again in three days. If you are the Son of God, come down off the cross and save yourself." He could not come down off the cross because the cross was the destruction of the temple that would be built in three days. This is the nature of the Lamb at its highest peak. He humbled himself to death to fulfill the will of God (John 9:28, KJV).

Of such were the apostles also. The entrance of physical death builds the kingdom of heaven. John, viewing the New Jerusalem adorned as a bride coming down out of heaven, saw twelve foundations with the names of the twelve apostles. It had twelve gates with the names of the twelve tribes of Israel. It also had great and high walls, wide and tall. As the gates are named after the apostles and gates after Israel, I believe the bricks or stones in the walls are believers in Christ.

Jesus's response to such cruel behavior in which he could see, but his disciples were blinded to, was "Rejoice and be exceeding glad: for great is your reward in heaven: for so persecuted they the prophets which were before you." In Acts 5, Peter and the apostles were beat for preaching the gospel. They went away rejoicing, that they were counted worthy to suffer shame for the name of Jesus.

This is the final level of maturity, and at this level, the believer is endowed with the character of Christ or the nature of the Lamb. It is this character that allows the believer's name to be recorded among faithful heroes (Hebrews 11:1–40, KJV).

Now the spiritual house is totally complete. It has been totally decorated by God. The world marvels at the distinct detail that God has woven into the house. Satan is so outdone that he tries everything he can to demolish the house. It can't be torn down until its mission and purpose is complete. When Satan finally gets the chance to tear the house down through death, he literally builds the kingdom of heaven. At death, the believer is physically in the Kingdom of Heaven and receives great reward.

Lesson 4–The Attitudes of Maturity

- Peacemakers – the ability to see through present conditions to the end of peace with God, promise of seeing God, eternal security
- Persecuted for righteousness sake – adorned with Christ's ways and distinguishable from the beast, residence in the kingdom of heaven, Revile, persecute, say all manner of evil against you falsely- Pressure to stop God's will – Great reward in heaven

Tests, Trials, and Tribulations

I would like to share a little about what I call the three Ts: tests, trials, and tribulations. Tests come to make sure we have received spiritual information. Trials come to see if we have the information in application. And tribulations come to stop the will of God in a mature Christian's life.

In the foundational attitudes, we develop the spiritual characteristics that will allow us to receive the knowledge of Christ. In the developmental attitudes, spiritual knowledge is accelerated. It comes from the inner seat of hunger and thirst. Tests come to make sure the believer has obtained spiritual knowledge. In Matthew 4:3–11 (KJV), Jesus was tempted or tested by Satan. What was tested here was the knowledge of God in the Son of Man. This is the same thing that happened to Adam and Eve in the Garden of Eden. Satan tested what Eve knew first. She indicated that she had received the knowledge. She stated that God had told them not to eat of the tree of knowledge of good and evil. She failed because the knowledge obtained was not applied. Jesus succeeded because he not only displayed that he had the knowledge but also applied it.

Trials come to make sure that we are able to apply the knowledge that we have received. God wants to see if our responses to natural situations will be according to his word. The Developmental Attitudes endow the believer with the characteristics of Christ, which enables them to make it through their trials.

In order to capture the essence of trials, we must turn to the Gospels. It is here we see the disciples sitting at the feet of Jesus to learn the ways of God. It seems as if Peter was the only one who acted out at times, for which Jesus corrected him. I imagine there were other incidents that are not recorded. A prime example of a trial would be when Peter denied Jesus. You have to take into account that Peter had told Jesus that he was ready to die for His sake (Luke 22:33, KJV). This would be the trial of his life. Jesus, understanding exactly where Peter was in his development, says, "You will deny me three times before the cockcrow." Even though Peter would fail this trial, Jesus prayed for him that he wouldn't fall all the way back. He told Peter that when he was converted to strengthen his brethren. This did not mean that Peter was not a disciple of Christ. He was converted when Jesus said, "Come follow me"; and he left everything to do so. His conversion here would be to move all the way into spiritual maturity. Even though we may fail in our trials sometimes, it is the very failure that catapults us into our destiny. It takes the proper developmental process to take a failure and turn it to victory. If Peter did not have the proper foundation, this trial could have made him turn away from the kingdom of heaven.

Tribulations are a little more difficult than tests and trials. The source of tribulations can come from God or Satan. When tribulations come from God, it is in the form of chastisement for persistent disobedience. Tribulations also come from God as the birth pains of his wrath and final judgment. The other side of tribulations comes from Satan. When an individual reaches maturity in Christ, Satan tries to stop their mission. His attempting to stop the work of God is tribulation. Developing Christians experience tribulations from God for disobedience. It is only the mature Christian who experiences tribulations directed from Satan. Despite the enemy's attempt to stop God's plan in your life, know this: no weapon that is formed against you can prosper. Many are the afflictions of the righteous, but God delivers them out of all.

This process aesthetically and uniformly brings the spiritual house to its final product. The believer is endowed with the nature of the Lamb. His life is in God's hands. At which point Paul said, "For me to live is Christ and to die is gain." The mature believer's life becomes another stone in the temple at death.

Lesson 5–Tests, Trials and Tribulations

- Tests- Does the believer have the information?
- Trials- Does the believer have the information in application?
- Tribulations- Is the believer going contrary to the will of God? Satan is trying to stop the will of God in the believer's life.

PART 2

The Characteristics of a Godly Man

Characteristics of Christ

Ephesians 5: 23–27 (KJV) says, "Husbands, love your wives, even as Christ also loved the church, and gave himself for it; That he might sanctify and cleanse it with the washing of water by the word, That he might present it to himself a glorious church, not having spot, or wrinkle, or any such thing; but that it should be holy and without blemish." I think the key that begins to unlock the mystery of godly men is the phrase "Husbands, love your wives, even as Christ also loved the church, and gave himself for it."

Despite the fact this phrase speaks to the married men, it transcends every part of manhood. "Husbands, love your wives even as Christ loved the church." The big question is how did Christ love the church? Indeed husbands are married to wives, which implies Christ is married or espoused to the church. The answer: he gave himself, which means he literally died for the church. Therefore, a husband loves a wife by giving himself.

For years, I've asked God to expound on giving oneself as a husband and how to love one's wife like Christ loved the church. The answer lies within the relationship Christ has with the church. It is found randomly throughout the New Testament. More specifically, it is found in the book of Revelation, in the direct interaction Christ had with the church.

Revelation 1 gives us descriptions of Christ. In these descriptions, there are two questions that uncover his character. One, what does Christ say about himself? Two, how does John describe him?

What does Jesus say about himself? "I am Alpha and Omega, the first and the last, saith the Lord, which is, and which was, and which is to come, the Almighty" (Revelation 1:11, 17-18 KJV). John heard the voice of the Lord. It sounded like a trumpet. He heard the Lord speak, saying, "I am the alpha and Omega, the first and the last."

After John had fallen as a dead man, Jesus touched him and identified himself as the first and the last: "I Am he that liveth, and was dead; and, behold, I am alive for evermore, Amen; and have the keys of hell and of death" (Revelation 1:17-18).

Next, let's look at John's description of Jesus. His first interaction is with the Spirit of God. He said, "I was in the spirit on the Lord's Day" (Revelation 1:10 KJV). The next interaction is with the voice of the Lord. It sounded as a trumpet. He turned to see the voice that spoke to him. He saw seven golden candlesticks, and in the midst of the candlesticks was one like the Son of Man. The Son of Man was clothed with a garment down to the foot. He was girt about the paps with a golden girdle and had a head and hair as white as wool. His eyes were as a flame of fire and feet were like brass as if burned in a furnace. His voice was as many waters. He had seven stars in his right hand and a sharp two-edged sword coming out of his mouth. Finally, his face shined as the sun.

Now let's list what Jesus said about himself: I am Alpha. I am Omega. I am the beginning. I am the end.

I am he which is. I am he which was. I am he which is to come. I am the Almighty. I am he that liveth. I am he that was dead. I am alive forevermore. I have the keys of hell. I have the keys of death.

Let's list what John saw: I heard a great voice as a trumpet. I saw seven golden candlesticks. I saw one like unto the Son of Man. He was clothed with a garment down to the foot. He was girt about the paps with a golden girdle. His head and his hairs were white like wool. His head and his hairs were as white as snow. His eyes were as a flame of fire. His feet like unto fine brass as if they burned in a furnace. His voice was the sound of many waters. In his right hand, there were seven stars. Out of his mouth went a sharp two-edged sword. His countenance was as the sun shineth in his strength.

Jesus instructed John to write to the seven churches. His writing is a dictation from the mind of Christ to the church. The church can be looked at in a couple of ways. One, we can look at it as the universal church that include those who died in the faith looking for the promise, the saints that have gone on before us from the inception of the church to we that are alive now. Another way we can look at the church is in periods that characterizes the church. For the sake of this book, I will be looking at the latter of the two since each period characterizes the church. There are seven periods for which Jesus names churches. According to the Law of Moses, if a man died not leaving seed with his wife, then his brother should take her to wife to bring seed for his brother. Apparently, it could be up to seven brothers. The Sadducees give reference to this in (Matthew 22:23–28, KJV). I think it ironic that they mentioned seven husbands and in Revelation Jesus mention seven churches, which can be characterized as seven wives. Since the periods are consecutive, the same Law of Moses would apply.

In this book, Jesus characterizes himself with each church. The lists above can be looked at as the characteristics of Christ. He is the husband, and the church is the wife. While speaking to each church, he mentions something of his character. His interaction with the church characterizes the God-man. At least one attribute of his character from Revelation chapter one is expressed to each church.

The seven churches are Ephesus, Smyrna, Pergamos, Thyatira, Sardis, Philadelphia and Laodicea. In this book the name of each succeeding church will be the espoused wife of Jesus Christ.

- To Ephesus he says, "I am the one which hold the seven stars in my right hand and walk in the midst of the seven golden candlesticks" (Revelation 2:1 KJV).
- To Smyrna he says, "I am the first and last, was dead and is alive" (Revelation 2:8 KJV).
- To Pergamos he says, "I am he that has the sharp two edged sword" (Revelation 2:12 KJV).
- To Thyatira he says, "I am the Son of God which has eyes as a flame of fire and feet like fine brass" (Revelation 2:18 KJV).
- To Sardis he says, "he has the seven spirits of God and seven stars" (Revelation 3:1 KJV).

- To Philadelphia he says, "he is holy, true and has the key of David. He opens and closes doors" (Revelation 3:7 KJV).
- To Laodicea he says, "I am the Amen, the faithful and true witness, the beginning of the creation" (Revelation 3:14 KJV).

Ephesus, the Virgin

Control

I look at Ephesus as the church in its infancy. She is a pure virgin cleaned by the work of Christ and undefiled by Satan. Jesus identifies himself in two ways with her: First, as the one that holds the seven stars in his right hand. The idea here is that Jesus has been with the Father and is clear as to his direction and purpose. The church as the wife is there to help accomplish his God-given mission. This is the characteristic of control. I know that the word *control* brings alarm to the female mind. Many relationships operate on manipulation and control instead of love. The hand of Satan is at the root of both. Insecure men compensate by brute control, driving his relationships with fear. Women involved in relationships like that learn to manipulate for their survival. That is not the type of control I'm talking about. A godly man has to have control in every area of his life. He must have control of his physical body, spiritual life, emotions, work, and family.

Jesus is aware of what belongs to him and where they are. He said that he held seven stars in his right hand. They belong to him, and he is in control of them. Despite the fact that he is in control, the seven stars, which are the leaders of the seven churches, are still at liberty to move at their own free will. The Old

Testament was a schoolmaster to people of the New Testament. We are supposed to look at what happened in the past and make better decisions for our lives. In the dictation of the seven churches, we have the voice of wisdom speaking to us loudly, yet our ears have become dull. When Jesus wrote to the seven churches, he gave insight into their future. Had the stars been able to use his words as a schoolmaster, some things may be different in our world today. They had the freedom to move and shape, but instead of moving they fell into the ruts of the words of Jesus. So the control that Jesus exercises on the church is not forceful but loving, even though he knows and expresses fate if she doesn't catch the clues he has left her.

Lesson 6 – Control

- A godly man is defined out of his relationship with God. It gives him direction and prevents indecisiveness. When a woman is involved, she plays a role in his definition.

Control of the Physical Body

Godly men are in control of their physical bodies. They have been blessed by God to have a physical drive for procreation. This can be seen in God's command to be fruitful and multiply (Genesis 1:28, kjv). He also told the woman to be fruitful and multiply. The same command translates differently to men than women. God does not handle them the same. A good example would be Matthew 19, as Jesus responded to the Pharisees concerning a divorce issue saying, "And I say unto you, Whosoever shall put away his wife, except it be for fornication, and shall marry another, commiteth adultery: and whoso marrieth her which is put away doth commit adultery." Here the one reason a man could divorce his wife is fornication. Without this exception, marrying another person would constitute adultery and with the exception the divorced woman should remain single. There is something unspoken in these words that define men and women. Evidently, Jesus knew something about women when he implied they should remain alone having been divorced. There is a part of womanhood able to exercise control by allowing that part of her life to lie dormant while focusing on a higher purpose. In this case, you have to look at the audience Jesus had, which were men. After hearing that a divorced woman should remain alone, one of them spoke up, saying, "What if the case is with the man?" His response was speaking directly to the fact that sexuality in men is different from women. He says, "All men cannot receive this saying, save they to whom it is given" (Matthew 19:11-12 kjv). Therefore, their responses to singleness will not be the same. Understanding this, it is imperative that single, godly men and women be developed by God, and then move into a committed/married relationship.

The apostle Paul instructed his son in the gospel to flee youthful lusts (2 Timothy 2:22, kjv). This is good instruction for young people. Run for the Lord, while fleeing youthful lusts. Men flee by channeling their energy into constructive behavior. Women flee by holding a standard of chastity. The idea comes from two chains of thought. One, the husband, Christ is looking for a chaste bride. Ephesians 5:27 KJV Two, the parable of ten virgins. Five were wise and five foolish. The five wise virgins kept their oil while the foolish used theirs. When they went out to buy what they lacked, they missed the opportunity to be a bride (Matthew 24:1-13 KJV).

Chastity is a protective cover for women. It saves them from abuse and helps them to enter marriage. When a man finds a woman he is looking for procreation. If a woman enters a procreation relationship without marriage, she opens her life for abuse. Chastity makes the man decide if he really loves her and want to marry or move on. If he marries her, she has what she has been looking for. If he moves on, she does not have the abuse and mistrust from the relationship.

Lesson 7 – Control of the body

- Men exercise control by linking to God. He has a window to operate in before God's command to procreate points him to a woman. This window is different depending upon the temperament of each man. To remain in the will of God, the godly man purposefully looks for a committed relationship with a woman.
- Godly women exercise control by maintaining chastity. By taking her focus off procreation and redirecting on a higher purpose, she is able to maintain.

Control in Your Spiritual Life

In all that we know about predestination and purpose, the greatest asset to spiritual development is growth. Blind growth in some cases is better than prophetic destiny. So many times, words are prophesied over people. These words cause them to search for a destiny through prophetic voices. There are so many people that have been misguided by that process.

Matthew 6:33 says, "But seek ye first the kingdom of God and his righteousness and all these things shall be added unto you." It is the process of growth that reveals the fruit of a tree. Likewise, it is the process of spiritual growth that reveals God-given purposes and destinies. There are two elements of spiritual growth spoken of in verse 33. One is the entrance into the kingdom, and second is to seek his righteousness. Once one enters into the kingdom through Jesus Christ, one must seek after the righteousness of God. Despite the fact one may have entered the kingdom of God, the dysfunctional attitudes caused by the beast have to be dealt with. After Israel had been delivered from Egypt, Moses was on the mountain receiving new living instructions from God. The people reverted back to what was in them. They built idols to worship which stood in the way of their destiny. Therefore, divine purposes and destinies are prefaced with the ways and knowledge of God.

As God dealt with Israel, he is going to deal with godly people. He is not going to leave them in their dysfunctionalism. Godly people have to be careful and watchful as to catch themselves before reverting to their old ways or finding comfort in dysfunction.

What I mean by blind growth is growing in Christ without knowing purpose or being overly concerned about it. The process itself grows purpose and destiny.

The Second Epistle of Peter 5:5–8 (KJV) says, "And beside this, giving all diligence, add to your faith virtue; and to virtue knowledge; and to knowledge temperance; and to temperance patience; and to patience godliness; and to godliness brotherly kindness; and to brotherly kindness charity. For if these things be in you, and abound, they make you that ye shall neither be barren nor unfruitful in the knowledge of our Lord Jesus Christ." Godly people have to diligently and purposefully develop their spiritual lives.

They must submit to spiritual authority such that they can be taught the word of God. They have to keep themselves in a place to hear the word of God. Matthew 6:33 says all these things shall be added to you. What things? According to the text, what you shall eat, drink, and wear. According to 2 Peter 1:5 (KJV), add virtue, knowledge, temperance, patience, godliness, brotherly kindness, and charity. These things make you spiritually fruitful.

A godly man and woman exercises control in their spiritual lives by the awareness of the growth process and where they are in it.

Lesson 8 – Control in Spiritual Growth

- The godly man has to plant himself in the house of God such that he can grow.

In Control of His Emotions

A godly man must understand or come to understand who he is and how God has designed him. This understanding leads to healthy man emotions; emotions that are different from women's; emotions that are God given and not woman assigned.

There is a concept in the Bible that I call the rule attitude. It comes from Genesis 3:16 and basically says that the man shall rule over the woman. This was given as a corrective measure for disobedience to God's law. Misinterpretation of what God meant has led to extreme abuse of womanhood. Through time, men have used it to lord it over women even to the point of treating women as simple livestock. It began in Genesis 4:19 when Lamech took two wives. It is more readily seen when dowries were instituted to compensate for the loss of a daughter. When Abraham sent his elder servant to get Isaac a wife, he sent a dowry or compensation to Rachel's father for his loss. We also see it when Jacob worked for Rachel and Leah for fourteen years to compensate their father for his loss. We see the ultimate in King Solomon having seven hundred wives and three hundred concubines (2 Kings 11:3). So there was a general concept that women were possessions of men. It was never the will of God or his intent for women.

Any suppression of God-given freewill at some point is going to be challenged. I believe the women's movement is the challenge to suppressed womanhood. I support the movement of womanhood for equal rights. However, in the midst of equal rights, there is a redefinition of manhood. Womanhood began to define manhood out of its suppressed state. Really, manhood is defined by God, and womanhood is found in manhood. In Genesis 2, God creates the man and totally defines him and sets his environment. When Adam was looking for a comparable being to himself, she was found within (Genesis 2:20, KJV). As womanhood began to redefine manhood, it assigned emotions to manhood that it did not understand. They defined men to be more like women. To get the proper scope of the emotions of manhood, we have to go back to its originator, God. A brief look at the creation of man and woman tells us a lot about the workings of manhood and womanhood. It would do us well to note the environment God created for man to live in. It was a place where he found definition. It included shelter, food, water, wealth, occupation, and instruction. Even though man dwelt there, it was not so much for man as it was for woman. So the environment God created for man was really for woman. Women also create an environment for man, which will be seen in the scenario that follows.

The external or physical makeup of manhood and womanhood can be defined by comparing the skeletal bones of the arm and ribs since woman was made from a rib. The arm bones are relatively hard compared to the rib bones. The arm bone, being outside, represents man, and the ribs inside, woman. This scenario defines man as externally hard and woman externally soft. During a boxing match, boxers always cover their ribs with their arms because the arms can take the hit whereas the ribs will be bruised easily. Therefore, a man protects and covers his wife in the external realm. In the physical environment, he provides a safe environment for his wife.

The inner workings of manhood and womanhood can be seen by comparing the rib cage to the vital organs. The rib cage, being inside of the body, and the vital organs inside of the rib cage define the inner workings of men and women. The rib cage represents womanhood, and the vital organs, manhood. It represents women are internally hard and men are internally soft. I know that a lot of men don't want anything to do with the word *soft*, but the godly man must understand how he is made such that he can articulate what he needs for survival. As a matter of fact, biology has determined that men and women both have male and female traits. Secular knowledge alone has led us astray, and much confusion abounds because of these definitions. But really, there is nothing feminine about men or masculine about women. The soft part of men is just as masculine as the tough part, and the tough part of femininity is just as feminine as the soft part.

There are some things in God's creation that can't be understood by science alone. One is how the human body can be regenerating in some aspects yet dying at the same time. It takes the word of God to bring sense to it. Therefore, some definitions can only be established through the word of God, which is able to distinguish between soul and spirit (Hebrews 4:12, KJV). I feel that male and female are two of the things that can only be defined by God. The external toughness of man provides protection to the externally softness of woman. It creates normal conditions such that the rib cage can focus on its function protecting the vital organs.

Even though God created Eden for Adam's environment, it is not what solely sustains manhood. The rib cage creates a safe environment for the vital organs to function. The rib cage represents womanhood, and the vital organs, manhood. The vital organs are the most vulnerable parts of the body, yet they play a major role. They are the lifeline of the body and part of a never-ending circle of give-and-take.

These simple principles of men being externally hard and internally soft, and women externally soft and internally hard, unlock the secret to the actions of men and women.

Abuse happens to women when they don't understand the internal working of men or themselves. Generally, men are no match for women in the arena of words and remembering sequences of events. At the onslaught of words and events, he moves into a state of being closed up. This is normal and necessary for survival. Some men, when pushed too far, respond in ways that they know will help them win—in the area of physical strength. The result is physical abuse to the woman. The internal softness of a man is no match for the internal hardness of a woman. Likewise, the external softness of a woman is no match for the external hardness of a man.

In a world of divide and conquer, women have become less than what God had intended for them. Now, living in a time of equal rights, women are defining their own environment. In this redefinition, men should be more attentive and show more of their emotions. The problem with this scenario is that womanhood is all wound up because manhood did not provide an environment conducive to her well-being. Now womanhood is on the rampage, and what is inside of her is real, but it is not right. The worst part of all, manhood is not aware enough of what is going on with her, to help her unwind so that she can see the truth. In Genesis chapter three, God says the woman's desire shall be to her husband and he shall rule her. This did not mean that man would use woman as a possession but guide her desire when it gets outside the perimeters of the Word of God.

A case in point would be crying. Women generally cry a lot more than men. That should not be the guiding factor as to say men are insensitive. There are parts of man that are not readily seen. It is the softness of womanhood and manhood that brings tears. Since that part of womanhood is out, her tears are readily seen. The tears of manhood can't be seen because they are internalized. Sometimes when men don't understand what they need to cover their softness, they can become calloused. Their softness is locked away or "closed up" for which tears may never come out of their eyes. However, when they understand and have the proper covering, there are moments in life that pull at their heartstrings which bring tears. Just because water doesn't come out of his eyes doesn't mean he is not crying. So the key is not to make men more sensitive like women as to cry but to understand them for who they are. The redefinition of manhood by overwhelmed womanhood is destroying our society. The man that we see today is not a man defined by God, but man that is defined in the eye of emotionally strapped womanhood. To see him and the deception makes me sick. Not only am I sick of it, but womanhood is sick because it hates what it has created in the long term. Therefore, many characteristics of manhood are not God designed but woman assigned.

As stated the enemy is working to destroy the family. One of the tactics he uses is the confusion of man and womanhood. The simple understanding of man and womanhood as God has designed answers the corroding family.

Lesson 9 – Emotions

- Men designed internally soft and externally hard – men's emotions are internalized, not readily seen
- Women designed externally soft and internally hard – women's emotions readily seen

In Control of Work

A godly man is a worker. The Bible teaches if a man doesn't work, he doesn't eat. It also says if he doesn't provide for his family, he is worse than an infidel (1 Timothy 5:8, KJV).

Colossians 3:23 says, "And whatsoever ye do, do it heartily, as to the Lord, and not unto men." We must put our best efforts into all that we say or do, including our work.

A godly man is a worker that will receive promotion. Promotion doesn't come from anywhere but the Lord. When you work as unto the Lord instead of men, your godly decorum makes you an asset to your employer. You come to learn the process and value of obtaining and holding a position. He also learns to build upon small things.

A good example of a godly man in the Old Testament is Joseph. The Bible doesn't show the frustrations of Joseph. We get the idea from reading the story that he is a positive kind of person, and his godly decorum causes him to prosper no matter where he is. Joseph was a free man with destiny and purpose in his heart. He didn't know when, where, or how, only that he would be an instrument to bless his family in the future.

Joseph was sold into slavery and landed in Potiphar's house. He showed integrity, and he fled youthful lust when Potiphar's wife propositioned him. He fled, and that was the right thing to do. But that situation landed him in prison unjustly. His godly decorum caused him to rise in Potiphar's house and the prison. As he worked in prison, his gifts were uncovered, and he became an interpreter of dreams. Joseph built on small things. He had a job in Potiphar's house and a job in prison. The jobs he had in prison allowed his gifts to be uncovered such that he would be prepared to do the job of his destiny. Despite the discomfort of prison, they were stepping stones to take him to his destiny.

In the African American community the allure of fast money through selling drugs has deceived many young men. The enemy has injected the thought, "I am not going to work for minimum wage by flipping burgers." In turn, many are automatically enlisted in Satan's army by selling drugs, which destroys the family unit. On the one hand, they understand that they are taking care of their individual families. That is honorable. On the other hand, they are destroying the family unit at large through what they do. The lies that Satan has fed them will ultimately destroy their individual families when they are incarcerated or dead. They don't understand the God-given concept of work, and the enemy wants it to be that way.

God wants to do the same with you as with Joseph. Greatness is found in smallness. God resists the proud and gives grace to the humble. Therefore, you have to start working somewhere regardless of how small. That could be the place where God will allow you to uncover the gifts he has instilled in your life. Once Joseph's gift was discovered, it took him to the top. Not only was he able to provide for his family, but also for nations.

A godly man must understand the process of work and development of vocation.

Lesson 10 – Work
- Build on small things and discover your gifts.

In Control of His Family

A godly man is a family man. God told Adam to be fruitful and multiply and replenish the earth. I want to explore this command from two perspectives: before the fall of man and after the fall. Before the fall, this command could only mean men were married to women, producing fruit, which fulfils the command. After the fall, the command is affected differently. God is the same and his intention is the same, but Satan has other ideas. Men still marry women and produce fruit, but there is another dynamic working. Genesis 4:19 (KJV) says, Lamech took two wives. The enemy started to distort the will of God. In the time we live, marriage is dying, and people are cohabiting now. The fruit of these relationships raise the spectrum of societal problems and dysfunction.

A godly man has to have good understanding in at least three areas for a Christ-centered family. He must have a good relationship with God, his wife, and his children. The correct understanding and interaction proven over time raises leaders and provide a stable society (1 Timothy 3:5).

His Relationship with God

When God constructed Adam, it is apparent that he was first in Adam's life. But because the earth is populated, males are more likely to get in other relationships before they connect to God. The God-first principle provides a male with the necessary tools to grow into a godly man.

Adam's relationship with God before he came in contact with woman gave him the tools to carry out the will of God . In Genesis 2, God created Adam and gave him life. He then placed him eastward in the Garden of Eden, which gave him shelter. He told Adam to eat of the trees, which gave him food. There was a river that flowed from the garden, which gave him water. There were gold and precious stones on one of the rivers, which gave him wealth. He told Adam to dress and keep the garden, which gave him his occupation. He told him not to eat of the tree of knowledge of good and evil and to eat of all the other trees, which gave him instruction. He told him to name all the animals, which set him in dominion. After Adam was defined, God gave him a wife.

When a man has a relationship with God first, he will be equipped for life. Living in a distorted and imperfect world, it is hard for men to get God first. If men would raise their sons to contact God first, a new generation of leaders will arise. They will transform the face of the corroding family.

Lesson 11

- Spend time with God for his definition of your life.

His Relationship with His Wife

Out of everything that God provided for Adam, the only thing that he actively pursued was a counterpart—a woman, a wife. The most prized of all gifts to man is a woman. There was no way that Adam could carry out God's instructions without her. He must understand who she is, how she is created, and what it takes to support her spiritually, physically, and emotionally.

Spiritually, he has to maintain the instructions given by God despite the presence of the woman. This was one of Adam's failures. He quit listening to God and started listening to his wife, who had been influenced by Satan. There is nothing wrong with a husband listening to his wife as long as she is influenced by God. Under God's influence, she is a builder of his kingdom. The determining factor is if her words and actions are aligned with what God says . If they don't, a godly man must understand that he has to cover his wife. Numbers 30:6–9 (KJV) says, "And if she had at all an husband, when she vowed, or uttered ought out of her lips, wherewith she bound her soul; and her husband heard it, and held his peace at her in the day that he heard it: then her vows shall stand, and her bonds wherewith she bound her soul shall stand. But if her husband disallowed her on the day that he heard it; then he shall make her vow which she vowed, and that which she uttered with her lips, wherewith she bound her soul, of none effect: and the Lord shall forgive her." Yes Eve did eat the fruit. But if Adam, being with her, would have spoken up and followed God's instructions,

Eve and humanity would have been spared. In this fashion, his wife would have been covered.

Part of the problem with most men is that they have not been with God long enough to receive instructions for their lives.

Physically, he has to understand that his wife needs to be covered by his strength. He has to be able to take the hit in order to protect her and the family from danger. Strength is not only physical; it is also the ability to stay put even when there is nothing one can do about a situation. That's called going through it together. In the godly man's mind, the outcome will be the will of God, and everything is going to be all right.

We are all emotional creatures, but God has designed women to be the portal of life, and their emotions or feelings are at an elevated level. Under normal conditions, women give birth to healthy life, but when pressures bear down on them, sometimes abnormalities come along with that life. A godly man has to keep her conditions normal so that she can continue to produce healthy fruit in every aspect.

When her conditions are not normal, she can become overwhelmed or emotionally strapped. At this point, she is going to birth chaos. When a woman is pregnant, she understands that what's inside of her is real. The baby that she feels inside is real and adds another dimension to her womanhood. I call it her base of feeling. It not only works in pregnancy but every aspect of her life. She can have ideas growing in her emotions and in her thoughts. For instance, when a woman meets a man that has potential, she has already pictured marriage and what the children will look like. The man has only said, I like you. She does this out of her feeling base. If she gets to a place where she is overwhelmed, what is inside her can be as real as God's word. This is where a godly man must cover his wife—by maintaining normal conditions such that she will not get to a place that overwhelms her. In Genesis 3, the serpent tested Eve's knowledge of God's word. He used reverse psychology and said, "Hasn't God said don't eat of all the trees in the garden?" She corrected him, saying, "We can eat of all the trees except the one in the middle of the garden." So her knowledge was intact, and Satan was not going to fight her in a knowledge battle. He had to arouse her curiosity by saying, "You will become like gods, knowing good and evil." This caused her to take another look at the fruit. Her sight equated the fruit good for food. But when she took it or touched it, she moved totally from her base of knowledge to her feelings. Based upon what was now inside of her, it was all right to eat. On the part of Eve, there was nothing wrong with that. She was being a woman. Adam was at fault because he didn't speak up and cover her. There are at least two things that can make a woman move from her knowledge base to her feeling base. First is the allure of Satan, and second when her husband doesn't give her the proper environment for womanhood. The awareness of the godly man and woman are crucial here.

Lesson 12

- A godly man supports his wife spiritually by covering her with the word of God.

His Relationship with His Children

The godly man must understand the importance of his fruit—offspring or children. Ideally, children should be the fruit of a marriage union. It is great to be able to carry on your family name and to leave a legacy. But the most important part of offspring is the preservation of God in a generation (Genesis 18:19). God is speaking of Abraham, saying, "For I know him, that he will command his children and his household after him, and they shall keep the way of the Lord, to do justice and judgment; that the Lord may bring upon Abraham that which he hath spoken of him." One of the reasons for Abraham being chosen is that he would systematically put God into his children to maintain the way of the Lord.

Psalm 127:3–4 says, "Lo, children are an heritage of the Lord: And the fruit of the womb is his reward. As arrows are in the hand of a mighty man; so are children of the youth." God is preserved in children, and it is the godly man's responsibility to make sure that his children are God's. Verse 4 speaks of a mighty man. To be a mighty man, one must have obtained some degree of accuracy with his arrows. Otherwise, he would not be a mighty man but a dead man. The term "mighty man" is suggestive of war. To fight the fight that has been waged against the family, the godly man has to point his children with precision in a way that causes them to be aligned with the will of God.

He provides for, protects, and directs his children. The hardness of his manhood or physical covering of his wife brings the same protection to his children. The softness of his manhood brings provision to his wife, which in turn covers his children.

When a husband understands and provides the conditions that God gave Adam in the Garden of Eden, it makes an environment for a healthy wife. When a wife understands and provides safe conditions for her husband's softness, she creates an environment for a healthy husband. A healthy environmental manhood and womanhood produce children that are God-ready. God-ready children are the offspring of these relationships. They are ready to be used by God at an early age.

There are two major keys that God has given to the godly man for his children to come out God-ready. First is correction. The Bible says, "Who the Lord loves, he chastises." Correction calculates in the heart of a child as love. Second is direction. The godly man, like an arrow, must point his children to accomplish the will of God.

Lesson 13
- The keys to children are direction and correction.

Presence

The second, way Jesus identifies himself to the Ephesian church is as the one walking in the midst of the seven candlesticks. One way you could look at it is that the candlesticks are giving him light. In this aspect, the candlesticks are providing the means for him to operate in the earth. Another way you could look at it is that he is maintaining the candlesticks. Rather than look at it from a standpoint of either-or, we should look at them together. First of all, they belong to him; therefore, he is the initiator, and what the candlesticks provide is a result of his initiation. Being in the midst of the golden candlesticks shows that his presence is there all the time. We know that his presence is there all the time because in Revelation 2:5, he said if Ephesus does not repent, he will remove her candlestick. This suggests he is present and aware.

Speaking of presence, there are two areas I want to deal with: the physical presence and the presence of God.

Physical Presence

In Matthew 28, Jesus gives the great commission to the church. In the later part of verse 20, he says, "And lo I'm with you always even unto the end of the world." It is the assurance that no matter what we encounter on this Christian walk, he is going to be right by our side. Despite how easy or difficult the situation is, he says, "I am right here." For some reason, men have a tendency to hide when something doesn't go right. I suppose it is the delicate part of their manhood that doesn't want to be exposed. Similarly, Adam hid when he had gone contrary to the command of God. The character of Christ teaches men to stay in place.

A godly man's presence must be felt in his family all the time whether he is at home, work, or recreation. His wife has learned to trust his actions. He has a track record of returning, and the threat of abandonment or brief AWOLs are absent from her mind. If the wife has come to know this, the children will also. Not only do they come to know, but they will operate in it. It brings security and stability to his family.

One of the plagues of the modern family is the absence of husbands and fathers. It breeds unruly and ungodly children, absent and void of the ways of God.

Lesson 14

- Faithfulness in presence gives stability to the family.

The Presence of God

One of the dynamics of candlesticks is they have a need to be lit and maintained in order to be beneficial. Jesus is in the midst of the candlesticks as the high priest, and he is the one that ignites and maintains the light or glory of the candlesticks. His ability to ignite and maintain the candlesticks comes from his relationship with his Father. Being in the presence of his Father gives him the illumination that is needed to navigate through a dark, sinful world.

John, speaking of Jesus, says his head and hair was white as snow, and his countenance was bright as the sun. This is the direct result of being in the presence of his Father. He was imbued with the presence of God to the point that his countenance emanated like the sun with the glory of God, and his head and hair appeared as white. Moses spent forty days with God on Mount Sinai. When he returned to the children of Israel, his face shone as the sun. He had to be veiled so that people could be in his presence. It is spending time with God that brings purity and the glory of God to the godly man, and it gives him direction.

Lesson 15

- Personal time with God consecrates and gives direction to godly men.

Smyrna Destitute

Strength of Character

Smyrna represents the second phase of manhood. Her environment was hostile. She was fighting and fearful for her very life. If Jesus is who he says he is, why didn't he take her out of this situation? Instead of taking her out, he said it was going to get worse. Jesus wanted the godly man to understand that there are times when he has to go through. Some things he goes through can't be paid with money. A doctor, lawyer, or banker can't help in these situations. There are two keys the godly man must pick up here. One, Jesus says I am the first and the last. It is an indication that he is going to be with you all the way. He is not going to bail out. The godly man has to learn how to stay with it and not bail out. Because of the way we are designed, we have the tendency to hide when things don't go right. This is what Adam did after he had fallen. He hid. He bailed out. Many of us do the same thing, but Jesus is saying, "Don't bail out, I am right here with you. I am the first, meaning I am going in with you. I am the last, which means I am coming out with you." That should be interpreted as you are coming out without a shadow of doubt.

He told Smyrna she was going to be tested for ten days. A ten-day test is a test of the flesh. It determines your staple diet. Daniel 1:12 (kjv) says, "Prove thy servants, I beseech thee, ten days; and let them give us pulse to eat, and water to drink." Rather than eating the king's meat, which was offered to idols, Daniel chose a test of ten days to see if they would be fairer and fatter than the other soldiers. The test of ten days was to see if the church would take meager to no provision and stay with the Lord or sell out and indulge in the delicacies of Satan.

The second key, he says, "I was dead and am alive." He is saying, "I have been to hell and back. I am still here." Jesus told the church at Smyrna to stay faithful even to death. The ten days of tribulation would kill off the flesh such that the wealth of the spirit could be manifest. The death of the flesh brings the life of the spirit.

To the Smyrna church, Jesus did not offer to pull her out, but he gave her the strength of his character. There comes a time in a godly man's life when he has to die out to the flesh. There are times when you don't know what to do or where to go to get help. You even go to Jesus, but it seems as if he is not coming through for you. The ultimate act of love is that a man would lay down his life for his friend. Testing time determines whether one will really lay down his life for the sake of the gospel.

In the times we live, it seems as if money is the answer to all problems. The idea is if you can come up with enough money, everything will be all right. There are some basic elements to human existence that cause one to be satisfied. They are food, water, shelter, companionship, and obedience to the will of God. Money can definitely buy more food, water, and better shelter, but it can't buy obedience to the will of God. I'll tell you what can bring you into obedience: tests. For example, Peter thought that he was ready to die for the sake of Christ. Jesus told him that before the cock crows, he would deny him three times. It was not his initial words that brought obedience but the test of denial.

The godly man must possess strength of character when tough times come. No wife or child wants to go through a time of testing which can embarrass or humiliate. But it makes it easier when a family can go through a test together. The godly man has to be there in testing times to let his family know everything is going to be all right. His wife and his children need to be assured. Even though he does not have the answer in his hand, he has to have the understanding that it is going to be all right. He needs to hold his family in his arms and say it's going to be a rough ride, but we are going to make it. Just stay with them.

How can he say it's going to be all right and doesn't see an answer in sight? He has to know God. All things work together for good for those that love the Lord and are called according to his purpose (Rom. 8:28). "I am with you always even unto the end of the world (Matt. 28:20). I am the first and the last, which was dead but am alive forever more" (Rev. 1:17).

Just being there shows strength of character and brings stability and security to his wife and children. Despite the lack of basic needs and the test, his wife and children will remain emotionally and mentally stable. Sometimes women need to pin things down such that they can move on. For instance, in the case when she meets a possible partner and there is a mutual attraction, she will ask a question. Do you love me? She asks because she wants to pin down the relationship such that she can move forward. It is the same way in any crisis of relationship or life. She wants to pin things down or know where it is going. Women that do not understand this concept about themselves can become mentally and or emotionally disturbed if she stays in that condition too long. Single women need to learn how to finalize loose areas in their lives, especially if they has children. The mental and emotional disturbance can be passed on to the children. The godly man also understands this concept from the words and character of Christ saying, "I will never leave you" (Matt. 28:20).

What is it that causes the godly man to be able to stand firm and have grit and internal fortitude? It is the pattern of faithfulness and righteousness. John saw Jesus clothed with a garment down to his foot and wearing a golden girdle about his waist. A white robe represents adornment in righteousness. The garment along with the girdle represents priestly attire. Isaiah 11:5 says, "And righteousness shall be the girdle of his loins, and faithfulness the girdle of his reins." Isaiah, speaking of the coming Messiah, says he will have righteousness to gird his loins and faithfulness to gird his reigns. Loins and reigns are both ascribed to the area of the body below the rib cage and above the waistline. Righteousness represents the visible loins while faithfulness represents invisible reins, which are the inner controls or the guide of the core.

Therefore, faithfulness is the guide to righteousness. Matthew 6:33 says, "But seek ye first the kingdom of God and his righteousness and all these things shall be added unto you." One must first seek to be in the kingdom of God. It is accomplished by accepting Jesus Christ as Lord and Savior. The next step is to seek righteousness. It is accomplished by the addition of the word of God and the Spirit of God to the believer's life (John 6:35, 7:37–39). Blessed are they that do hunger and thirst after righteousness (Matt 5:6). It is a blessing to have an awakening of righteous hunger and thirst. The full grasp of righteousness in a believer's life comes through faithfulness to the word and Spirit of God. Therefore, faithfulness is the guide or reins for righteousness. It comes precept upon precept and line upon line (Isaiah 28:10). In order to gain righteousness in daily living, it takes being faithful as the Spirit of God leads you into all truth.

As we speak of righteousness at the core of a believer's being, it is satisfied by two agents, the word and the Spirit of God. Whenever you see righteousness, you should automatically understand word and spirit. Jesus, speaking of the Spirit, says, "Out of your belly shall flow rivers of living water." With the flow, there is the fruit of the Spirit. Therefore, the strength of his character is found beyond his natural ability, and it taps into God. Hence, we understand the concept that there is no shadow of turning in God (James 1:17, kjv). "Great is thy faithfulness" Lamentations (3:23, kjv). This characteristic alone is invaluable to the family, first to the wife and spilling over to the children.

Lesson 16

- In time of testing, don't bail out. Stay with your wife and children. They need your strength.
- The godly man's internal fortitude linked to God enables him to enter, go through and come out of the tests and trials of life.
- Women have to finalize loose areas of their lives.
- Faithfulness is the instrument that causes righteousness to be established in a godly person's life.

Pergamos Compromised

Decisiveness

The church in Pergamos was facing very difficult times. Its very survival was at stake. It was here that Satan's seat was positioned. The church faced martyrdom if it didn't participate in pagan worship and trade practices of the time. Antipas was a faithful servant who chose to stick with the ways of Christ and was martyred for his stance.

There were two forces working in this church that would push to one of two outcomes and maybe a third. The third could not be recognized because of compromise. The first force was persecution. Persecution happens when there is a belief system that goes contrary to the current establishment. The ways of Christ were adverse to the Roman culture and rejected by Jews. An uncompromised stand here would bring persecution and a certain death.

The second outcome was compromise. In this case, compromise was a marriage between two different ideologies that caused the adverse parties to exist together. This was the route that the church chose. It was accomplished by an old tactic fostered in the heart of a hireling prophet name Balaam. Balaam had been off the scene for some period of time, but his cunning had been adopted by a man named Nicolaus. Nicolaus adopted the same methodology or doctrine of Balaam to bring compromise for the existence of the church. Of course his leadership was not what the church needed at the time. It is so unfortunate that in times of vulnerability, the wrong type of leader shows up at times.

The story goes like this: (Numbers 22:1–25:8 KJV) Israel was claiming the land of Canaan and, with the help of God, defeating all they came in contact with. King Balak saw what he was up against and devised a plan to defeat Israel. He hired the prophet Balaam to curse Israel so that he could gain victory. When Balaam tried to curse Israel, the word of the Lord came saying, "What I have blessed can't be cursed." Of course those words put a wrench in the plans of King Balak and a dent in the pocket of Balaam. Here we have a people that God had blessed and couldn't be cursed. But despite this, Balaam finds a way to cause Israel to be cursed for monetary profit. Namely, they had to curse themselves. It was accomplished by causing the men of Israel to fornicate with Moabite women, merging the two cultures. This made God turn from Israel. As a matter of fact, twenty-four thousand Israelites were destroyed by God as a result of the merger.

Nicolaus used the same tactic with the church in Pergamos. He caused the church to compromise or merge for provision.

The other avenue that could have been opened is by going through the persecution. God fights for the meek (Psalms 76:9, KJV). Some lives may have been lost, but God would have to show up to fight on their behalf. A case in point is the three Hebrew boys, or Daniel in the lion's den. They refused to compromise, which caused the boys to be thrown in a fiery furnace and Daniel in the lion's den (Daniel 3; 6). By taking a stand, they allowed God to fight on their behalf. By compromising, the church has allowed Satan to put a wedge or seat in the church that undermines the true power or wealth of God. Earthly wealth, for which the church compromised, is slowly and systematically removing the power of God from the church. If the church would have gone through without compromise, the church would be much different now.

The husband that Jesus appears to be in this church was as the one with the sharp, two-edged sword coming out of his mouth. The first observation is that the sword, which is usually in a soldier's hand, is coming out of the mouth of Jesus. This is suggestive that the fight is not a physical fight but a fight of ideologies, specifically those of Christ and Satan.

The godly man must fight to be true to Christ and maintain the ways of Christ in his family. With the onslaught of information in our time through the information highway, it is easy for people to fall into areas of ungodliness in their secret encounters on the Internet. Pornography abounds and many ungodly thought processes are out there. Through the word of God, men must distinguish between good and evil and cling to the good.

Hebrews 4:12 (KJV) says, "For the word of God is quick and powerful, and sharper that any two-edged sword, piercing even to the dividing asunder of soul and spirit, and of the joints and marrow, and is a discerner of the thoughts and intents of the heart." It is vital for a godly man to be armed and filled with the word of God. It is through the word that his decision process flows. First of all, the word is alive and quick. It is powerful and able to perform what it says. It is able to cut to precision the ways of Christ and Satan. In the Pergamos church, the ideologies were so mixed that the common person could not distinguish them, but the sharp two-edged sword could. In the account of Balaam and Balak, it was the sword of Phineas, piercing through an Israelite man and a Moabite woman committing fornication, that stopped the plague of death. Even now it is the precise use of the word of God that can fix any problem in Christian relationships. The godly man must be able to make decisions based on the word of God.

In doing a word study of the three parts of man, it was easy defining the body. But when I began to define the soul and spirit, I had trouble because the same Hebrew and Greek words that define the word *soul* in many instances are the same as *spirit*. I came to the conclusion that there are two sides to mankind, the physical and spiritual. The physical is flesh and the spiritual consists of soul and spirit. The flesh and spirit are opposites. The soul is the center between flesh and spirit. So the soul fades into the flesh but is readily distinguishable. Also that the soul fades into the spirit but is not easily distinguished. They are so intertwined, it takes a precise instrument to separate them: the word of God. There are many instances when the godly man will be faced with obscure circumstances. If he leans on the ideology of the time, man can fall out of the will of God. If he uses the word, he will separate Satan's plans and bring to plain view the will of God for his family.

When the church could not distinguish between the teachings of Nicolaus and Christ, the sharp two-edged sword brought clarity for the right decision.

It is imperative that the godly man engage in the study of God's word for the proper guidance and leadership at all times, especially times of obscurity.

There will be times in every godly man's life when there is a conflict in direction between his wife and him. Because of the way women are designed, she will want it finalized. She can rush the husband to one of her logical resolutions. It may or may not work. The godly man must not be anxious but step back and take time to seek God before he comes to a decision based on the Word of God. This process reveals compromises and leads the family to true spiritual wealth.

Lesson 17

- The godly person has to be watchful of areas the enemy can offer compromise. Compromises are recognized when the believer is seemingly at a dead end. The compromise substitutes true spiritual wealth for worldly wealth.

Thyatira, the Influenced Mother

Jealous

The church in Thyatira represents the fourth level of manhood. A deep deception was at work in the church, which was affecting the most important part of the church—its children. Contaminated children take humanity away from God. Even though we know there was growth in the previous churches, there was no direct communication of its children. But with this church, there was a direct mention of children. They are called Jezebel's children, but they are really the children of the church that have been taught by Jezebel. Jezebel was a spirit which, at that time, could not birth children. This spirit had to have live and intelligent offspring to thrive.

It's the same concept used in Genesis 3:15, speaking of the offspring of Satan and the offspring of the woman. The offspring of the woman and the offspring of the serpent both came from the woman. The offspring of the serpent are the children born to humanity and the seed of the woman is Jesus Christ. Satan is also a spirit being; therefore, he does not have offspring. So through compromise the spirit of Jezebel thrive in the children of the church.

Jesus identifies himself in two aspects with this church—the one with eyes as a flame of fire and feet of brass. These two aspects of his character show grace and judgment. His eyes are as flaming fire because he has been put in a position where he has to fight for the affection of the church/wife and his children. The church in Thyatira had become enamored by the person of Jezebel, which in turn affected her children.

The part of his character that was showing was anger and jealousy. Exodus 34:14 says, "For thou shalt worship no other god: for the Lord, whose name is Jealous, is a jealous God." Therefore, one of the attributes of God is that he is a jealous God. What does it mean to say that God is jealous? God is many things. God being jealous simply means that he wants what belongs to him . He demands faithfulness from the objects of his love. This simple principle teaches us that the ideal relationship is one husband and one wife. The attitude is carved right out of the heart of God. Any other idea of multiple husbands, wives, or same sex unions is something less than what God had intended for humanity. The God part of man instinctively makes him jealous over his wife or family when their affections are turned in another direction. Despite his rage, he shows grace to Jezebel by allowing her space to repent (Rev. 2:21).

There is another side of jealousy that watches over as in protection. This is what makes men protectectors of their families.

The second characteristic, shown to the church in Thyatira, is his feet of brass. A godly man must be able to show mercy and the grace of God such that his family can be saved. Despite the good qualities of grace and mercy, there have to be times when a godly man executes judgment. The person and character of Christ in the dispensation of grace extends a hand such that whosoever accepts him can be saved. The time will come when grace will no longer be extended, but free-moral agents that have exercised their will against God will have to experience another side of God, which is judgment. As Jesus dealt with Thyatira, he extended grace but after grace was extended judgment came (Rev.2:22-27). Despite the failures of his wife and children, a godly man must not be quick to execute judgment. He has to allow space for repentance and restoration.

Two ways that feet are expressed throughout scripture are oppression and deliverance. Isaiah 18:7, says, "In that time shall the present be brought unto the Lord of hosts of a people scattered and peeled, and from a people terrible from their beginning, hitherto; a nation meted out and trodden underfoot, whose land the rivers have spoiled, to the place of the name of the Lord of hosts, the mount Zion." Through Israel's disobedience, they had been scattered among the nations, indicative of them being under the foot of their enemies. Being underfoot means being in a place of judgment, and a godly man must come to know the time and season to put things under his feet.

He gave Jezebel and those that she influenced a chance to repent showing his mercy. If they didn't repent, they would fall into the judgment of the serpent's head bruised by the foot of Jesus (Genesis 3:15).

When he shall put all things underfoot, it will be feet of brass that will break the hardness of the nations and those who did not fall upon the stone (Luke 20:18).

Another way feet is portrayed in the Bible is through the concepts of deliverance and salvation. Isaiah 52:7 says, "How beautiful upon the mountains are the feet of him that bringeth good tidings, that publisheth peace; that bringeth good tidings of good, that publisheth salvation; that saith unto Zion, Thy God reigneth!" The feet of Satan brought sin and captivity, but the feet of Jesus and those he sends bring deliverance.

The godly man has jealousy in his eyes to vigilantly watch over what belongs to him along with feet of brass that will execute judgment at the proper time. When Adam disobeyed God in the Garden of Eden, God did not deal with the situation immediately. He waited till the evening because Adam had turned in another direction. Adam's disobedience aroused the wrath of God, but God did not deal with Adam in his wrath; he waited until he had calmed down (Genesis 3:8). A godly man seeks to deal with life's situations out of the cool of the day. He must not be hasty to move against the disobedience of his objects. Decisions made in the heat of the moment can cause unwise judgments that can have far-reaching complications.

When God created Adam, he gave clear guidelines as to what Adam could and could not do. The range of what he could do extended far beyond what he could not do. As a matter of fact, there was only one thing he could not do, and that was to eat of the tree of knowledge of good and evil (Genesis 2:17). The eyes of God were very watchful of the actions of his objects, and the instant Adam went in another direction, immediately, the fire of jealousy came into God's eyes. God had given good instructions, and the consequences of what would happen were very clear (Genesis 2:17).

God had to deal with the situation, and the consequences were severe: they should die. But God, in his mercy had a plan to recover Adam and not destroy him. So the judgment of God was tempered with love such that he could recover his loss.

A godly man follows the pattern God has put before him in his family dealings. Jesus followed the same pattern when dealing with the church in Thyatira. His jealousy was aroused, causing his eyes to flame. Not only did his eyes flame, but his feet of judgment cast in brass were also showing. His feet of brass represented the harshest judgment for the transgression committed. In between his eyes of flame and his feet of brass was his heart of love. He gave the church space to repent and a chance to be recovered.

With the enemy fighting against God's ideal for marriage, many men find themselves locked out of God's best for them. After ruining the opportunity with the women of their dreams, many men are just drifting from relationship to relationship. I think the church's judgment in these matters is sometimes extreme, exacting the fullest punishment upon individuals. After all, the Bible says, "Thou shalt not commit adultery" (Exodus 20:14). One thing I know about the law is that it is blind. In one case, the judgment fits the crime, but in other cases, it is either too hard or soft.

Laws within themselves do not have a heart of love and mercy, whether it is of Moses, the government or individual homes. A godly man must be aware of this and allow space for repentance such that his family and people can be recovered.

When men and women enter into marriage without God and the understanding of what God wants for them, the marriage can end up in divorce. Many men haven't taken the time to know themselves, much less women . Their driving force is God's command, "Be fruitful and multiply and replenish the earth" (Genesis 1:28).

Without God's understanding for marriage, a man can end up in internal conflict. Once going through a failed marriage, the fire of manhood can be extinguished. This is where the conflict lies. God said first of all, "Be fruitful and multiply" (Gen. 1:28). which is a command or drive to encourage procreation. Secondly, he said, "Thou shalt not commit adultery" (Ex. 20:14). The man has a failed relationship along with a God-given drive to be with a woman. The damage from the failed relationship makes him hide from returning to marriage. God's command is driving him to satisfy his flesh. The marriage commitment is a spiritual thing, and the drive is a natural thing. Not having the spirit or the wisdom of God guiding him, the physical drive wins out. The man settles to live with God's command be fruitful and multiply outside will of God. The disobedience makes him hide from God in one aspect while fulfilling God's word in another. He really needs to have the correct relationship with God, which instructs him to marry such that procreation can be legal. The conflict causes him to either go from woman to woman or to cohabit settling for simple release from woman. Design makes him choose release from the creature, woman.

This conflict put men in what I call play mode because he is hiding. Any woman involved with him can look forward to settling and being mishandled. There is a way that women can protect themselves and that is to maintain chastity with him. Do not give him what he wants. It will cause one of two things to happen. If he really loves her, he will enter marriage. If not, he will leave her alone. Really, this should be the rule of every woman that wants to be married. Men have learned the concept of overpowering women to get what they want especially men raised by single mothers. To win at this game, women have to do a couple of things. One, she has to know herself by pin-pointing her triggers and setting limits for each of them. Two, she has to maintain a mystique about herself. When limits are set, never operate near your limit. Your design as a woman will help you. Sorry, but I am a man partial to women in dresses. When a woman puts on the right dress that fits her physique, shoes, purse, hat, and all the accessories, it gives her a mystique. She can't be too revealing but there has to be a hint that there is something really good in her package. Her persona must say, I have something that you want but you can't have it unless you marry me. I can't speak for other men but a woman like that gets my attention. The way she puts it together will attract the right kind of men.

I work as a contractor . I was doing repairs on one of my Christian brother's home. After settling the contract and getting the work started in general conversation, he made a statement that came out of nowhere. He said, "God does not treat sexual sin the same." I was pondering in my mind where that came from. Why did he say that? I didn't respond to it because I think sin is sin, and God doesn't distinguish between sins, great or small. All sin stems from Adam's disobedience. The penalty of breaking God's law has to be paid. It will be paid by resolving all sin in the same place, the lake of fire. The only way we can escape this penalty is to accept Jesus Christ as our Savior. Deep down, I really knew why he said it. He was trying to reach out to help me in his own way. In my community, the people that really know me understand that before I went through a failed marriage, my reputation was impeccable for being faithful and staying with one woman. I guess he was trying to get me to loosen up.

There are many good sayings in our world, but not all good sayings are God's word. What this brother was expressing to me was seemingly a good saying, but simply not the truth. The truth of the matter is that God does not handle men and women the same. He handles them according to his design as men and women. He treats them equally but handles them differently.

A case and point is when the Pharisees came to Jesus questioning him about divorce (Matthew 19:3–12). They asked him if a man could divorce or put away his wife for any reason cause because Moses had allowed them to get divorces. Jesus reaffirms in the word of

God, that one man should be married to one woman, joined as one by God and allowing nothing to put space in the union. Jesus went on to say, "And I say unto you, whosoever shall put away his wife, except it be for fornication, and shall marry another, committeth adultery: and whoso marrieth her which is put away doth commit adultery." Simply, this woman should remain alone until she or her husband dies or reconciles.

His audience, being all men and knowing the command of God in their lives, speak out, saying, "His disciples say unto him, if the case of the man be so with his wife, it is not good to marry." Since they asked that question, let's change what Jesus said to what the disciples were thinking. Let's add the masculine to everywhere the feminine is in this verse to change the case scenario. "And I say unto you, whosoever shall put away her husband, except it be for fornication, and shall marry another, committeth adultery: and whoso marrieth him which is put away doth commit adultery" Simply stated, a divorced man should remain alone until his wife or he dies or if there is reconciliation. Since the audience were men, the statement was questioned because in the mind and constitution of the average man, that is impossible.

Jesus answered by saying, "All men cannot receive this saying, save they to whom it is given. For there are some eunuchs, which were so born from their mother's womb: and there are some eunuchs, which were made eunuchs of men: and there be eunuchs, which have made themselves eunuchs for the kingdom of heaven's sake. He that is able to receive it, let him receive it."

He says that all men can't receive this saying. In other words, men are not designed to do that. They are designed and commanded to be fruitful and multiply. On the other hand, women in general can receive this saying. Generally speaking, the vast majorities of men couldn't and women could. Also, there would be a small percentage of women that couldn't and men that can. So Jesus treats them with the same love and attention but handles them according to their design.

To say that God does not handle sexual sin the same is not a true statement because the wrath of God is going to be revealed upon all disobedience. The truth of the matter is that God does not handle men and women the same in this area. Also, men must realize they have to come to the Creator and quit leaning on the creation for support. Men who have been through broken marriages need to come to God for healing, definition, and restoration. Then he can quit hiding and move into a committed marriage and let God's command be satisfied according to his will.

If a godly man is married to a woman who departs from him, he has to give her space for repentance. This is what Jesus did with Jezebel and the children she influenced. When repentance doesn't come, there is a certain look for judgment. The temperament and maturity level of the godly man will be a guide as to how long the space should be. All men can't receive this saying. Once a space for repentance has been allotted and the need to be with a woman is leading the man into disobedience, it is time to move on, as you are entering into sin because of God's command. The godly man must do what is necessary to maintain his relationship with God.

Now, I just opened up another problem. I know there are many people in unhappy marriages looking for a way out. This is not the door out of an unhappy marriage. Did I just swing open the gates for people not happy in marriages to get out? No? The Pharisees asked Jesus if a man could divorce his wife for any reason? Jesus responded that only if the wife has committed fornication. So the only just reason a godly man can divorce his wife is because of fornication.

Even if the wife didn't commit fornication and the godly man ended in divorce, the character of Christ should be the character of the church. The character of God and Christ is to allow space for recovery, for the judgment is already set.

If the church closes the door through its rules and regulations, that person is faced with certain judgment, the lake of fire. And we know that the rules and regulations of the church have been carefully constructed based on the Bible. Therefore, they have to be right and adhered to.

Historically, the church has closed the door and left people on the outside with that certain judgment. When that happened it gave rise to the spirit of independence. Since those people could not be part of the church, they raised up their own church simply because this part of the character of Christ was not fully understood. The spirit of independence is an American creed, but it happened long before America existed. It happened because the church did not understand this part of the character of Christ.

The spirit of independence in one aspect is great because it allows people who have been rejected to enter the kingdom of God before judgment is exacted on the world. In another aspect, it is damaging because it undermines the lines of spiritual authority and the unity of the spirit. The independent mind is one that is not accountable. Spiritual authority demands accountability. When there is no accountability, spiritual authority is undermined. From that mind-set, there comes a chain of splintering. With each splinter there comes less spiritual authority. Spiritual authority transfers the power of God to everyone beneath it in its purest form (1 Corinthians 12:28).

The spirit of independence is really a spirit of rebellion caused by a church that had misrepresented the character of Christ. We can see this through the church of the Laodiceans, who locked Jesus out. The danger of the commandment-adhering church was that it fell short and locked people out. The danger of the independent church is that it goes far beyond Christ to the point where he can't exist in it. For this, his eyes are aflame and his feet are like brass.

Lesson 18

- As families go through trying times, there can be an allurement of external forces seeking to define the family outside of the character of Christ. During these times, motherhood can look to other sources that appear to be good.

The godly man has to be watchful to protect his wife and family and guide them to Christ if they get off track.

- Women wanting to marry need to package themselves and never give the man what he wants until she has what she wants.

Sardis Prostitute / Drug Addict

Insight and Control

I believe the church in Sardis represented the church at its lowest point. To this church, Jesus identifies himself with two characteristics. One—he that has the seven spirits of God, and two, he that has the seven stars. Here, the understanding of the seven spirits of God is needed to understand the character of Christ toward this church.

One of the more popular understandings of the seven spirits of God comes from Isaiah 11:1–2, which says, "And there shall come forth a rod out of the stem of Jesse, and a Branch shall grow out of his roots: And the spirit of the Lord shall rest upon him, the spirit of wisdom and understanding, the spirit of counsel and might, the spirit of knowledge and of the fear of the Lord." If seven spirits or aspects of the Spirit of God are listed, the Spirit himself is not one. Really in this verse there are six spirits listed: one, the spirit of wisdom; two, the spirit of understanding; three, the spirit of counsel; four, the spirit of might; five, the spirit of knowledge; and six, the spirit of the fear of the Lord. This verse can be made to work if you add the Spirit of God himself to the number to make it seven. John saw something that was seven in number. He called them the seven spirits that belong to God. I certainly agree that the Holy Spirit is all of them, and more than one of these could have been prevalent in each church.

I would like to propose another view in this book, which I think falls closer in line with scripture and the understanding toward the church. To come to this understanding, we have to take a look at the throne of God as seen through the eyes of those to whom it has been revealed. The throne was revealed to at least three people—Isaiah, Ezekiel, and the apostle John.

There are two viewpoints of the throne of God, earthly and heavenly. The earthly view is a more obscure view since heaven is opened and the person is viewing it from the earth. I call this an earth view of the throne. The heavenly view is when the person is taken to heaven to view it. The heavenly view is much clearer.

One thing I would like to note is that the revelation of the throne of God is relevant to the historical events of the earth. Eternity's past and future are not represented. The revelation of God's throne deals with the earth in time present, past and future. One of the ways that Jesus identified himself is as Alpha and Omega, the beginning and the ending. These words encapsulate time and show that his dealings are with the earth and man only.

Before Adam disobeyed God in the Garden of Eden, he was on a course, which I call the plan of God. Whatever that plan was, we don't know, because Adam veered from it. Adam is still in the plan of God, but it is God's plan of redemption . After the redemption of mankind and the visions are complete, mankind will begin afresh with the plan of God, the same as the children of Israel who had to go into the wilderness for forty years. The forty years corrected the failure of Israel to believe God. After the forty years, they started afresh to carry out God's plan of salvation.

The throne of God was revealed to Isaiah. He looked up to see the throne in the heavenly temple. It was high and lifted up, and his train filled heaven . Isaiah saw seraphim, which guard the presence of God in its stationary position. They cried to one another, "Holy, holy, holy is the Lord of Hosts." This is what I call the initial view of the throne of God. It gives us a glimpse of the heavenly beings in the clause "the Lord of Hosts." It transitions the spiritual realm with the earthly realm in the clause "the whole earth is full of his glory" (Isaiah 6:1–8).

Ezekiel had an earth view of the throne of God (Ezekiel 1:1). As a matter of fact, the throne came down, or was mobile (Ezekiel 1:4). Ezekiel didn't see anything above the throne of God. The creatures he saw were beneath the throne. I think the four creatures are significant in that there are four of them and they had four faces. The four creatures represent four quarters of the earth and four periods of world history. The eyes in the wheels and beasts represent the knowledge of God toward the earth's past, present, and future. The four faces are Israel's transition through history, or God bringing salvation to humanity in the midst of satanic dominion on the earth.

The apostle John also saw the throne of God. There is a difference in John versus Isaiah's and Ezekiel's visions. John was brought up to heaven, whereas Isaiah and Ezekiel were on earth. What he saw were the four beasts along with seven spirits of God. John saw a full representation of God's dealings in the earth with Israel and the church. They represent God's knowledge of the earth, Israel, and the church's past, present, and future. All the knowledge there is to know concerning the earth and God's plan of salvation is encapsulated in the four beasts and seven spirits of God: Israel through four periods of history and the church through seven periods of history.

Zechariah 3:9 says that seven eyes shall be upon one stone. Revelation 5:6 says that the lamb had seven horns and seven eyes, which are the seven spirits of God. That one stone and the Lamb is Jesus. Zechariah 4:10 says that these eyes are the eyes of the Lord through the whole world, which represent the omniscience of Christ throughout church history present, past, and future.

To reconcile the thought, John mentioned seven spirits of God, and we know that there is only one Holy Ghost. I looked at the agent that is at work in the earth. The Father worked in creation, the Son worked in redemption, and the Spirit of God worked through the church. He empowers us to be witnesses and to help. The Holy Spirit's interaction in time gave and left impressions as he dealt with the church through each period with the seven churches for which John described them as seven spirits of God.

When Jesus said, "I am he that hath the seven spirits of God,"Rev.3:1 indicated that he had perfect knowledge of the church. He saw and knew the past that landed the church in Sardis in its present condition. He also knew what his Father's perfect will was for the church. He knew what it was going to take to get the church out of that condition. There was no twist or turn that had escaped or could escape the knowledge of God, not even these writings .

As Jesus knows everything about the church and is not moved, the godly man must grow to understand his wife to the point that he is not moved by the condition she is in. There are at least two bases women operate out of, which are knowledge and feeling. A prime example would be the scene when Eve is beguiled by Satan (Genesis 3:1–7). The first thing Satan did was test Eve on her knowledge level by giving her a false statement. He said, "Hath God said, ye shall not eat of every tree of the garden?" Her knowledge was intact, and he could not fight her on that level. She said, "We may eat of the fruit of the trees of the garden: But of the fruit of the tree which is in the midst of the garden, God hath said, ye shall not eat of it, neither shall ye touch it, lest ye die." As a matter of fact, she gave Satan the clue when she added neither shall ye touch it. In God's original instruction, that clause was not there. Maybe Eve added it from the perspective of a woman understanding the nature of womanhood. The church in Sardis is at the bottom because it acted out of the feeling base and did a lot of things that seemed to be all right but was really against the will of God. Jesus could see that she was in her feeling base, but he could also see her knowledge base. It was weak but could still be seen. He said, "You have a little strength. Strengthen the things that remain" (Rev. 3:2). This church knows it is naked before the one with the seven spirits of God. She can not run a game on Jesus because he can vividly describe her total past as he did with the lady at the well (St. John 4:7-38). His perfect knowledge of her broke the cover or façade of her life. Jesus is not set back by the fact that she has had five husbands and has settled to cohabit in her present relationship. He still wants her in his kingdom.

Godly men and women have to be able to see where their spouses have come from and still want them. In the midst of colorful pasts, their strengths have to be identified and built upon. Exposure plus unconditional love creates the path for healing and the ability to move forward.

The second characteristic mentioned concerning this church is that he holds the seven stars. As previously stated, he is in control. This control has to do with his relationship with his Father. The enemy works through the weaker vessel to get to the stronger vessel. The godly man must be in control of his wits and understand how Satan works. He must learn how to maintain his godly decorum despite where his wife is. He has to have enough insight into womanhood and his family that he is not moved by what they are doing. When womanhood is in its feeling base, it can pull the man out of character. The godly man must maintain control in order to get womanhood back to her knowledge base.

In the section, In control of his emotions, I mentioned a concept call the rule attitude. It is a misinterpretation of God's word. When God gave correction to Adam and Eve, he told Eve she would have children in pain, her desire would be to her husband, and he would rule over her. Men, being under the influence of Satan and sin, took this correction far beyond where God had intended. They began to have more than one wife, which in turn caused them to lord it over women. Ultimately, it caused women to be treated close to the level of livestock. This can be seen in the Bible accounts of Abraham seeking a wife for Isaac, and Jacob seeking a wife as well. Even though it was acceptable in the culture of that time, a dowry simply was a payment to compensate a man for the loss of his daughter. Abraham's elder servant had camels laden with goods in payment for Rebecca, and Jacob worked fourteen years in payment for Rachel. This attitude is what I call the rule attitude. It is a satanic expression, which rode in on the wings of disobedience.

Here the correct understanding of the husband ruling over the woman is needed. It simply means that he will cover her when she gets into her feeling base. The original woman in her knowledge base has free expression of thought. She operates alongside her husband, carrying out God's instructions.

By sticking to the word of God, the godly man can recover his wife even if she does stray. It will be as if she never did it. Numbers 30:6–8 (KJV) says,

> And if she had at all an husband, when she vowed, or uttered ought out of her lips, wherewith she bound her soul; and her husband heard it, and held his peace at her in the day that he heard it: then her vows shall stand, and her bonds wherewith she bound her soul shall stand. But if her husband disallowed her on the day that he heard it; then he shall make her vow which she vowed, and that which she uttered with her lips, wherewith she bound her soul, of none effect: and the Lord shall forgive her."

When the godly man covers his wife, God forgives her for the actions she has taken out of her feeling base—that is if she is submissive to her godly man and eager to repent.

The same thing would have happened in the Garden of Eden had Adam not been pulled out of character and away from God's instructions. He would have covered Eve's fault, and mankind would have been saved. Jesus, the epitome of a God-man, did not allow himself to be pulled out of character nor veer from the plans of his Father despite the fact that his objects were displaced. The first man, Adam, failed, but the second man, Jesus, was victorious. We are saved. As a result, all men have the opportunity of salvation.

God's people were emotionally strapped because they were dispersed among the nations and in bondage. Despite that fact, he maintained who he was. God's people sided with the devil and crucified him. He maintained control even through death to save his people. To those that come to repentance, there is salvation. If they don't repent, they take their sins upon themselves, and the brass feet of Thyatira will break them to shivers in the time of judgment.

Lesson 19

- Godly people can't be moved by the knowledge of their spouse's past. This knowledge along with unconditional love create a path to recovery.
- A godly man must be in control and not moved by his wife while she is in her feeling base , but cover her.

Philadelphia Recovered Drug Addict

Clean, Real, and Wealthy

Jesus identified himself to the church in Philadelphia as holy, true, and able to open and close doors. This church was in a place of vulnerability. From Sardis, it had experienced the full spectrum of what Satan had to offer. Philadelphia represents a womanhood that had been mishandled and had distrust toward manhood. To move her, it was going to take someone out of the ordinary.

Jesus says, "I am holy." It simply means to be set aside for the use of his Father. Being holy also means to be clean. The only way a godly man can be made clean is through the blood of Jesus. A virgin is a type of holiness. A person has separated themselves to be dedicated to one for life. In that same line is marriage. A virgin is a prize for any man or woman entering traditional marriage. Considering Satan's influence on men, a virgin man would be a real catch for any woman.

After being mishandled by Satan, Philadelphia had to have someone out of the ordinary to bring her womanhood back to productivity. Let me explain what I mean by bring womanhood back to productivity. Generally, women that have been abused by men get turned off, especially if there is a track record of bad men in their lives. If she is converted to Christ, she can become married to the Lord and stay in a protective state. This kind of woman needs someone exceptional to bring her out of her protective state. She needs a godly man.

One of my little sayings is a man can't help being a man and a woman likewise. When a woman gets pregnant, the joy of a child growing inside is one of life's greatest experiences. However, the birth of the child can be one of life's worst nightmares. During the nightmare, the woman says, "I'll never have another child. I don't want to go through that again." But after the child is born and the precious life that was in her womb is now in her arms, she forgets the pain that she endured. This opens her up to do the same thing all over again. She can't help it because she is a woman.

The same thing happens to women when they go through abusive relationships. Sometimes on the outside looking in, we say, "Why does she put herself through that?" There is definitely something wrong with being abused, but she can endure those relationships because she is a woman.

The concept of having birth pains and forgetting work in every aspect of a woman's life. If she gets to a place where she is emotionally strapped, she can turn off, and at that point, she is gone. She says, "I'm never going to open myself to another man until I die."

After she is out and has a chance to heal, she can't help being a woman. She will enter a relationship again.

She will do it because she has a command over her life: to be fruitful and multiply.

Because of this simple principle, a godly man must realize he can't be moved by everything that comes out his wife's mouth. In her moment, she speaks what she is experiencing, but in the outcome, she wants what's best for her family.

Philadelphia represents this definitive part of womanhood. Sardis represents the totally abused woman. Philadelphia represents the woman that has come out of abuse and set in her mind never to get involved again. In order to get this type of woman unlocked, it is going to take a real man who is godly.

The second thing he says is that he is true. In the mind of Philadelphia, there was a deep distrust that came from being involved with Satan. Jesus has the answer to distrust: "I am true. I am a real man. I am the real deal" (Rev. 3:7).

Before I go any further, I'd like to share a thought about masculinity and femininity. Christ is in the place of the man, and the church is in the place of the woman. There seems to be a problem with the church because it is made up of men and women expressed in the feminine gender while Christ is expressed in the male gender. The indication would be that in the church, men are feminine or soft. But that is not the case at all. Satan uses the masculinity of men to do his bidding by shunning the very thing they need. We can see this by the gross disproportion of women versus men in church. Their interaction with Satan has caused them to be broken, abused, and distrustful. Therefore, it takes the same characteristics of Christ to recover men. So when Jesus recovers the church, he recovers men and women. Therefore, the church does not feminize men but restore them to their rightful position and condition in this world and masculinity. In our society, toughness is one of the marks of manhood. So there is a concept, that men have to be hard in order to make it in this world. Along with that is hard work, hunting, fishing, bar brawling and street survival. Whereas work, hunting and fishing are things that show the hardness of men, bar brawling and street survival are distorted areas of hardness. The purpose of man's hardness is not to be a stand alone, but to provide protection for his wife and children. The godly man has moved to strength under control which gives him an appearance of softness. His strength may not be seen in the streets or bars but it is felt in its proper place, the family. If his family is threatened, his strength will be seen. The wrong concept of hardness is alluring young godly women to get involved with men that have misplaced toughness. I see so many young Christian girls go after that type of hardness and get pregnant out of wedlock.

Once Jesus has recovered a man, there are a couple of things working. One, he has made him clean, and two, there is a change of heart. The godly man must understand that his salvation experience is only a window for his life to be recovered. This is true especially for men that are not married or have been divorced. Within this window, he has to take this time to be alone with God and allow God to make him a spiritual virgin. He also needs to gain the characteristics of a godly man during this time. This window will close shortly because he will need to fulfill God's command: be fruitful and multiply. His survival as a godly man will depend partly on how well he can handle his relationship with a committed woman. He needs a committed relationship with a committed woman to keep him from falling into the judgment of God while fulfilling the command of God: to be fruitful and multiply.

Jesus says, "I am true and the truth" (Revelation 3:7; John 14:6, kjv). The godly man is a man of faithfulness, honesty and integrity. These characteristics break the shell and erase the scars of distrust.

Jesus knows what it takes for Philadelphia to be recovered. He says, "I am holy and a virgin. I have set myself aside for you. I have been waiting on you." He is the answer to a seemingly unanswered prayer .

The third thing he says to Philadelphia is that he has the key of David to open and to shut (Rev. 3:7-8). In describing what the key of David means, I would like to go back to Adam in his original state. In Genesis 1:28, God told Adam to be fruitful and multiply, replenish the earth, and subdue it and have dominion over the fish of the sea and the fowl of the air and the beasts and creeping things. I am interested in the part that says, "subdue the earth." I may get in trouble here because of definitions, but I have to reveal what has been revealed to me. There are some definitions that we have today that don't go along with the scheme of what God is doing. Some of the definitions we have are derived from the scheme of what Satan is doing in the earth. *Subdue* is one of those words.

Before Adam had fallen in the Garden of Eden, God told him to subdue the earth. In its purest form, subdue can't mean divide, conquer, and subjugate people. That concept is, in essence, satanic. If Adam would have remained true to God and had not eaten of the tree of life, all humanity would have been forever righteous. Under this umbrella, there is no place for dividing, conquering, and subjugation of men and nations. So to subdue the earth has to mean something else. It simply means to make the earth do what it's supposed to do, and that is to yield fruit.

As men grow and come of age, it would be the responsibility of the godly man to make space in the earth for them. Under this umbrella, God has given every man space to make the earth do what it supposed to do—yield fruit. The yielding of fruit is the source of provision, which is necessary for the godly family to be sustained.

After the fall, the fruit of the earth was seized by Satan. It was his way to control humanity and manipulate them to his advantage in exalting himself above God. This is why the concept of a man controlling a woman with money is ungodly. It is birthed from the heart of Satan. So the seat of Satan is not a throne in some kingdom but the controlling of the wealth of the world. Therefore, Satan has the ability to open and close doors to provision. That is his seat. During the times of Smyrna and Pergamos, this is what was happening. Satan had opened the doors to all that followed his plans, but to true believers, the doors were shut. Pergamos sold out and went for wealth rather than Christ.

In my studies, I've noticed that there is no mention of spiritual fornication in the Old Testament. What I mean by spiritual is what is directed toward God. There is much mention of spiritual adultery. There is also much mention of human fornication and adultery. But even in all of the New Testament, there is no mention of fornication toward God until you get to Revelation. Revelation is the only book that mentions fornication toward God.

What is fornication? In the natural, it is a physical sex act outside of marriage whether that person is married or single (Matthew 19:9, KJV). Adultery deals with the marriage covenant. Fornication is the physical act that breaks the marriage covenant. In the case of married people, where there is fornication, adultery is right behind it. One of the reasons fornication isn't mentioned is because it is a physical act between earthly beings, and God does not fit into that equation. However, God is a covenant-keeping God, and departing from his covenant constitutes spiritual adultery.

As can be understood from Genesis 2 and 3, the husband and wife bring something to the marriage. They are both totally different, but they are equal in value. Men bring their provision, and women bring sex to the marriage. Within the marriage union, there is an unselfish trade between the two. The husband can't use money for control, and the wife can't manipulate with sex. Money for control and manipulation are satanic and are used among men and women out of God's perimeters of marriage. It is unfortunate that many marriages operate with satanic principles.

Spiritual fornication is only mentioned in the book of Revelation. It still does not mean a physical sex act, but it has taken on another connotation. Spiritual fornication is when the church accepts provision from Satan. Because sexuality is equated to provision, the idea of the church taking provision from Satan is spiritual fornication. In Revelation 17, John saw a seven-headed beast with ten horns, which represents the kings and nations of the world. Upon the back of this beast was a woman that had committed fornication with the kings of the earth, and the inhabitants of the earth were drunk with her fornication.

Usually when a person rides a beast, it represents that person has tamed the beast to do their bidding. The woman on the seven-headed beast represents womanhood influenced by Satan, and she came into existence when Adam listened to Eve and ate of the tree of knowledge of good and evil. Adam abrogated his dominion and his ability to subdue the earth. Satan seized Adam's assets through his wife. Eve was still a physical woman, but her actions produced a monster in the spiritual realm. It is through this process that Satan hoards wealth with those that follow him. For this, the love of money is the root of all evil (1 Timothy 6:10, kjv). This wealth is easily tapped into for the selling of the soul.

Understanding the source of the church's provision can constitute a true covenant with Christ or fornication with the devil. We need to understand the true provision of Christ. The key of David unlocks true provision from Jesus for the church. With it, he can open doors that no man can shut and close doors that no man can open. It also gives access to the treasures in the house of David. The treasures in the house of David is not only what has been accumulated through war, but it is tapped into the treasure stores of heaven.

The key of faith is the vehicle God has given to the church to access whatever it needs. An example of faith-appropriating provision is when the tax collectors were coming through and asked if Jesus paid taxes. Even though Judas was the treasurer, he must have had very little in it. Jesus told Peter to catch a fish, and the one he caught would have the money in its mouth. He displayed the ability to open a door and make the earth yield. Despite Satan's strangling hold on the wealth of the world, the godly man's provision is appropriated through faith.

In Matthew 4:8–10, Jesus closed the door when Satan offered him all the kingdoms of the world and their glory. First of all, how could Satan offer him all the kingdoms of the world and their glory or wealth? He stole the kingdoms through Adam's disobedience. He tried to catch Jesus in the same trap, but Jesus has the ability to close the door. He closed the door to give the church a chance to exist and bring salvation to humanity.

If this wealth was rejected, he had to have something else in mind. He told Peter in Matthew 16:1, "And I will give unto thee the keys of the kingdom of heaven: and whatsoever thou shalt bind on earth shall be bound in heaven: and whatsoever thou shalt loose on earth shall be loosed in heaven." This was a key that Peter was to use after his death to bind in heaven and to loose in earth. If you think about it, what in heaven needs to be bound? It is the will of Satan that is affecting the earth. What needs to be loosed in the earth? It is the will of God, which is in heaven and needs to affect the earth.

Jesus used the key when he was hanging on the cross. There were two thieves crucified with him. One of them said, "If you be the Son of God, get us out of this situation!" His statement showed that he didn't believe in Jesus. The other thief said, "We deserve punishment for our sins, but this man has done nothing." He asked Jesus to remember him when he comes into his kingdom. He said, "This day, you will be with me in paradise." So to unbelief, the door is shut, and to belief, it is opened.

The key of David is an instrument to the church that first of all opens the door to believers to enter the will of God and bring it to earth. Secondly, it gives the believer what is needed to survive in a satanic atmosphere. When Jesus opens a door or avenue of wealth in this world, it is primarily for the advancement of the kingdom of God. The believer is allowed to share in the wealth for his survival. For instance, Jesus told the story of a businessman who gave five, two, and one talent to his servants for growth and development as he took a long journey. The one that was given five gained five, and the one who was given two gained two. But the one that had one talent buried it in the ground. Within the time that he was gone, the first two men had to have some kind of way to sustain themselves while they were gaining profit. There had to be enough profit that came off those talents to give them a good lifestyle plus a profit to the owner when he returned (Matthew 25:14–30, KJV). Herein lay the secret to spiritual wealth opened by Jesus. The motive for wealth can't be personal. It has to be used for the advancement and maintenance of the kingdom of God. As doors are opened, the wealth will advance the kingdom of God. It will also sustain the workers of the kingdom. Matthew 6:33 says, "Seek ye first the kingdom of God and his righteousness and all these things shall be added unto you." Before making this statement, Jesus had expressed that the Gentiles look for what they wear, live, and eat, but that should not be the thrust of his servants.

I like to think of men as being material handlers. We don't produce anything; we simply distribute what God has made available to us. In that sense, men are conduits for God to show himself to the world. If we take a look at Adam in Genesis 2, we see that everything he had came from God. That included his very existence. All Adam had to do was handle everything God had given him. Had he not disobeyed God, he would have become a distributor of the things of God to his offspring. Therefore, a godly man is a conduit where God can pour out his blessing in the earth. He is also a conduit for his family.

There is no way humanly possible for a man to be everything he is supposed to be without God. He is deficient in every way. All that is needed to sustain a wife and family is impossible to have outside of God. When a man realizes that he is nothing within himself and submits to God, he becomes a godly man. All that he has in intelligence, skill, and wealth has come from God. He is a conduit. When God has an open channel to the earth, he will pour out his glory at will.

This open channel creates an umbrella for the wife and family to be sustained. It covers womanhood emotionally, financially, physically, and in every way. We as men like to think that we are taking care of our families, but it is really God moving through us.

Because the godly man is a conduit, the door is open to his wife to bear children, to be raised as servants of God. It also creates a healthy environment for the family. It allows the wife to stretch the full potential of her womanhood in being a helper.

He opens doors for his children by pointing them in the right direction. Psalms 124:7 says, "As arrows are in the hand of a mighty man; so are children of the youth." I am not much of an archer, but I do know the arrow must be on target, and you have to take into account the distance the arrow must travel. At longer distances, the aim must be higher than the bull's eye because gravity will pull the arrow off target. The release has to be slow and steady so as not to make the arrow change direction by jerking. The godly man discerns the skills and abilities of his children and points them in that direction. When it is time for them to fulfill their purpose, they are not kicked out but released slowly so that they can hit the target. It is more important that godly children hit their target now more than ever before. With the world moving swiftly away from the things of God, it is important that our children hit the target in their generation.

In Genesis 18:19, God said about Abraham, "For I know him, that he will command his children and his household after him, and they shall keep the way of the Lord, to do justice and judgment; that the Lord may bring upon Abraham that which he hath spoken of him." The idea is that the ways of God will be preserved in the next generation. Abraham commanded his household—in other words, he pointed the children in the things of God.

One other thing opens and closes doors for the godly man, and that is being under spiritual authority. Being under spiritual authority is more than receiving salvation. It is being in line with the system that God has set for the church. Ephesians 4:11–12 says, "And he gave some, apostles; and some, prophets; and some, evangelists; and some, pastors and teachers; for the perfecting of the saints, for the work of the ministry, for the edifying of the body of Christ." This sets the line of authority sets spiritual leadership.

This is a little off the subject, but it is relevant to the godly man. Since I mentioned Ephesians 4:11, I would like to speak briefly on the apostleship. One of the characteristics mentioned as Jesus spoke to the church of Ephesus is that she had the ability to discern true apostles. With this discernment, the church distinguished false apostles. With the lines of authority being severely distorted in today's time, there are so many people called apostles. I think I am safe to say the term *apostle* is nothing short of abused.

Where are the true voices that can distinguish between the true and false apostle? Maybe there is not a clear understanding as to the office of an apostle. First of all, it is the top of the church and should not be used loosely. One of the first criteria for the apostleship is the individual must be an eye witness of Jesus. Despite the fact that we are not contemporary with the time Jesus walked the face of the earth, one can still have an experience of seeing Jesus if he so chooses to reveal himself for a specific purpose. We know of one incident in which this did happen. This was with Saul, before his name was changed to Paul, at which time he received specific instruction from the Lord (Acts 9:3–7, kjv).

The next thing is that an apostle is one that lays the foundation to the kingdom. When the apostle John saw the New Jerusalem come down out of heaven, one of its characteristics was it had twelve foundations. The names of the apostles were on the twelve foundations. The indication could be that there are only twelve. However, Ephesians 4:11–13 says he put some in the church for the perfecting of the saints till we all come to the unity of the faith. The indication here could be that apostles are given by the Lord until he returns. Because of the abuse, one mind-set would say there are no more. The more reasonable mind-set would say Jesus is still giving this ministry gift as well as the others.

What is meant by a foundation layer is evangelizing areas where the gospel has not been preached. So with these two criteria, it is highly unlikely that one would elevate to the apostleship in the United States. Most of those we call apostles are simply overseers. However, in the structure of church, those that are the heads of reformations may be considered apostles.

A godly man understands spiritual authority and aligns himself accordingly. He is accountable to his leader even in a time of discipline. This type of character and alignment causes doors to open for the godly man. He has the support of heaven through his leaders. In Matthew 8:5–13 (kjv), a centurion came to Jesus on behalf of one of his servants that was vexed by palsy. He sought out Jesus to heal his servant. As Jesus was ready to go to his servant, the centurion spoke up and told Jesus to speak the word only. He understood what it was to be under authority and believed that his servant would be healed by simply speaking the word. He and the citizens understood that Rome stood behind him as he carried out his assignment. The godly man is the same way. Because he is under spiritual authority, heaven stands behind him as he carries out the will of God for his life.

Lesson 20

- Through his relationship with the Lord, the godly man is clean or holy. He is focused and looking for a committed relationship with the right woman.

- True provision of Christ comes by going through trials without compromise even in the face of death. This provision is appropriated through faith.

Laodicea Self-Sufficient Business Woman

Final Authority

Laodicea represents the church in its final stage. To this church, Jesus identifies himself as the Amen, the faithful and true witness and the beginning of the creation of God. This church had the brand of being self-sufficient. The course it has taken allows it to function in the world as a comparable entity with the institutions of the world. As a matter of fact, its structure and function does not resemble Christ at all, but the world system. Its pattern is corporate America, which is a source of competition to Jesus. For example, wealth has become a replacement for faith in many ways. The provision that Christ would bring is substituted by physical wealth and His healing by good job benefits.

This church indulged in spiritual fornication, and its wealth was maintained through the world system. In other words, it was stroking the breasts of the woman in the scarlet-colored dress sitting on a seven-headed beast with ten horns (Revelation 17:3, KJV).

Jesus greets this church as the church, "of the" Laodiceans. It indicates the church is being governed by the will of people. The United States for some reason is not mentioned in the Bible. It has become such a world power; how in the world could it be left out of significant Bible prophecy? One reason which I will talk about later is that the Bible is not the plan of God. It is God revealing the plans of Satan for the earth. It reveals Satan's dealings with the Old and New Testament churches. The Old Testament church is Israel, and the New Testament, the church. It is also God's plan of redemption for humanity.

The United States is of the people, by the people, and for the people. It is governed by people. The representation of Laodicea in the Bible is the United States. The church looks and acts just like it. This is another reason why spiritual or apostolic authority is compromised.

Jesus says to this church, "I am the Amen." Amen means "so be it." It affirms what has been stated is the truth. Usually Jesus speaks of himself as Alpha and Omega, showing the sequence of events. He says he is the Alpha, indicating a beginning point, and Omega, an ending point. It is interesting that he identifies himself as the end before the beginning in this case. He says, "I am the Amen, or I am the Omega," indicating that this church represents the end. Despite the church's self-sufficiency, he is still the final authority that sees all, knows all, and has all power. He is also Alpha and dictated the church's outcome, influenced by Satan, from its infancy.

When Adam and Eve disobeyed God in the Garden of Eden, the wrath of God was aroused toward humanity. When Eve partook of the fruit, their eyes did not come open, but when Adam ate, their eyes came open.

When God came in the cool of the day, he did not approach Eve or the serpent first but said, "Adam where are you?" It indicates that God made Adam the responsible person or the final authority.

Based on the word of God, the godly man must be able to make decisions that soar above womanhood when she is influenced by Satan. These decisions come by knowing what God has said and being obedient to it.

Speaking of the church following corporate America, I'd like to talk about the condition in the church that rivals Jesus a little deeper. According to our constitution, we have the understanding that all people are created equal. It is the right of every American citizen. Whereas I can see the merit in having such a creed, it is not instituted by God; it is the will of the people.

The idea of being equal, along with the fallibility of fallen humanity, has developed a mind-set that is contrary to Christ. The Bible does not teach that we are all equal, but it does teach we are all equally important. No matter what capacity we operate in, our function is vital to the survival of humanity and the kingdom of God. Therefore, the concept should not be equal humans, but humans that are equally important. 1 Corinthians 12:12–27 (KJV) lets us know that the body of Christ has many members that provide different functions. All the parts can't be the eye or the hand, or else the body would suffer. All the parts are equally important. This is the correct concept we should have of people. They are all different but are all equally important.

Since the church follows corporate America, the ideology of the church is that all humans are equal.

Therefore, women are equal with men. But really, they are not. Women are not men; therefore, they can't be equal and vice versa. They are only equal in importance and function.

The concept of equality is satanic, and its end is to destroy the image of God such that he can be like the Most High. It is birthed from satanic influence of wicked men with an insatiable hunger and thirst for wealth and power. It is the offspring of supremacy and slavery. I like to call it an illegitimate child that can never be fully accepted into the true family. Equality is two separate ideologies at war with one another. Supremacy says, "We are stronger and smarter, and we beat you. After all, the Bible says you will be servants." Slavery says, "This is inhumane, and we are people just like you. We don't deserve this in a land that is free." The answer is equality for all men regardless of race or creed. It has never worked from its inception. The constitution has been written, and the laws have been set. Deep in the minds of one segment of the population is the idea that we are better, and the other side is saying we are not beneath. Now there is a constant fight for equality. Along with it come programs for the disadvantaged such as social welfare and affirmative action. These elements are needed to strike a balance of equality, but all at the same time, they are destroying the family. People that worked so hard for nothing now will not work for anything. In other words, slaves worked hard at the hand of their taskmasters for less than food and shelter. Now that they are free, they will not work. Now we have government-subsidized housing ridden with unemployment, crime, and drugs. Why is it this way? Simply, equality is not a God-given principle. It is an idea birthed from people (Laodicea) under the influence of Satan, masters and slaves alike. The end is to destroy the image of God and ultimately overthrow God's throne.

Equality doesn't stop there. It goes on to men and women. The same hand is drawing the picture, and it is ever so clear. The face is not seen but the hand is well known. Men lord it over women, and why? Because the Bible says, "He shall rule over you." The influence of Satan on fallen man causes him to move away from God's original design and begin to herd women as livestock. The bible says, "Cursed be Canaan," therefore you are cursed and deserve to be subdued (Gen. 9:29). This injustice calls for equality of men regardless of origin. Now equality dictates that women have to be equal with men. Along with it comes the redefinition of manhood and womanhood and the escalation of sexual confusion.

Equality in turn dictates that people with same sexual preferences are equal, and now, it doesn't make any difference what the Bible says. This is because womanhood is in its feeling base. The ideologies feel right but are contrary to the word of God. So equality has taken us on a downhill slope, and who knows what it will dictate next? Maybe we should all receive a mark in our foreheads or hands.

Since these are some of the things that have happened in this country, the same thing is happening in the church for which Jesus says, "I am the final authority." I am the end of all this mess, and I can take corrective action.

The godly man has the proper concept of humanity. God created all of us equally important. God in his infinite wisdom made some men with a greater intellectual ability, others with mobile abilities, and finally those that have a degree of both. Some people have the knowledge about certain tasks, but do not have the skill to perform them. Some people are just gifted to do certain things without the study of the particular art or vocation. The intellectual is not greater because he can scientifically articulate how something is built, nor the one gifted to build greater because he can bring it into existence. The two are far separated and could never meet, so God created people with a balance of both to join the greatest skill with the greatest knowledge to produce the greatest product. Therefore, he created us all with a function or a place in humanity and in the body of Christ. The godly man understands that we are equally important.

There are two lines of authority that I want to mention here. They are both critical to the survival of a godly man. Without them, he ceases to exist. They are spiritual and family authority.

The lines of family authority are drawn from 1 Corinthians 11:3, which says, "But I would have you know, that the head of every man is Christ; and the head of the woman is the man; and the head of Christ is God." In this line of authority, Christ is submitted to God, man is submitted to Christ, the woman is submitted to the man, and children are submitted to their parents. This is a structure or pattern that God has set to establish the family. This is the only way it will work according to his plan. Even it has been influenced by corporate America because now everyone in the family has to be equal. The ideology is wreaking havoc in our families. Understanding the importance of function, the godly man and woman take their proper place in the line of family authority as provider and life-giver.

Spiritual authority is of initial importance, but I mentioned the family first because spiritual authority is also set within family authority. According to Corinthians, there is God, Christ, man, and woman in the line of authority. Within Christ are the lines of spiritual authority according to Ephesians 4:11–12. In the spiritual line of authority, there are apostles, prophets, evangelists, pastors, and teachers. The godly man should already be set under the lines of spiritual authority before he starts a family and be in it through his family. Ideally, he should have learned this in his parent's house and establish it in his house when he is married.

Why are the lines of spiritual and family authority so important? Let me explain. When God created the earth, he laid foundations, structures, and frames to cause everything that he created to function correctly. For instance, this earth and the sun are on a course set by God. It is on course by perpetual decree. Likewise is the sand on the seashore set by perpetual decree that the water will not overtake land (Jeremiah 5:22). There are patterns and frames all around us. We can't see them, but they are there. They are set by God such that the world will function as he designed it. Spiritual and family authorities are two patterns set by God such that the church and the family can function as he designed it. When anything moves away from the pattern or course that God has designed it, chaos follows.

Within the lines of authority comes the full support of God. Satan knows this, so he will do anything to break the power of God in this earth. Therefore, a godly man must be in alignment. When the lines of authority are crossed, it gives Satan the opportunity to destroy the image of God and cause rival with Jesus Christ.

The last thing he says to this church is that he is the beginning of the creation of God. The Bible says that all things were made by him and are held together by the word of his power. Despite the fact that the bride of Christ is in rivalry with him, he is cognizant of who he really is. This statement alone identifies the fact that there is an original design for his bride. Not only does it suggest, but it also leads the church back to that design. He is cleaning the church, such that it can be presented back to him without spot, blemish, or any such thing.

Let's explore the phrase "the beginning of the creation of God." In doing so, I would like to compare two terms in the Bible: "before the foundation of the world" and "from the foundation of the world."

When we think of the term "before the foundation of the world," we are speaking in reference to God outside of time. Outside of time, God is not referenced as beginning and ending because the terms are time sensitive and give reference points to time. Psalms 90:2 (KJV) says "God is from everlasting to everlasting." The indication is God has no reference as to his beginning or his ending. Therefore the term "before the foundation of the world" is only referenced or attached to God in infinity.

The term "from the foundation of the world" relates to time and what happens here on earth. Its references are beginning and ending or alpha and omega. Even when Jesus refers to himself as Alpha and Omega. He is defining himself in the scope of time. Luke 11:50–51 (KJV) defines the term:

> That the blood of all the prophets, which was shed from the foundation of the world, may be required of this generation; from the blood of Abel unto the blood of Zacharias, which perished between the altar and the temple: verily I say unto you, it shall be required of this generation."

The blood of the prophets shed "from the foundation of the world" was from Abel to Zacharias. It deals with the beings of time. Even Jesus spoke in relevance to time because he stopped at Zacharias because of where he was positioned in time. Therefore, when he says, "I am Alpha and Omega," he is only speaking of his human existence here on earth. This is why in Revelation 13:8, he says he is the Lamb slain from the foundation, not before the foundation. That is because the figure Jesus Christ is time sensitive and has no relevance outside of time. The relevance of Jesus Christ is a body to shed blood to appease the wrath of God.

However, his existence as the Word is outside of time. Jesus, speaking to the Father, said, "Glorify thou me with thine own self with the glory which I had with thee before the world was" (John 17:5, KJV).

John 1:1 (KJV) says, "In the beginning was the Word, and the Word was with God, and the Word was God." The First Epistle of John 5:7 agrees and says, "For there are three that bear record in heaven, the Father, the Word, and the Holy Ghost: and these three are one." In his eternal existence, he is known as the Word. Since we are contemporary with the character Jesus Christ, we retrospect this character to eternal past and project him to eternal future. From where we are, it is okay, but technically it is incorrect. In eternity past and future, there is no purpose for Jesus Christ the Son of God; the Word is the proper term. The glory that he had before was as the Word of God. The glory he had here on earth is the Son of God. Revelation 19:13 says, "And he was clothed with a vesture dipped in blood: and his name is called The Word of God." After dealing with the great whore called the Mystery of Babylon, he appeared as the one having his vesture dipped in blood and was called by his original name, the Word of God. Therefore, he returns to the glory which he had before, which is the Word of God. Understanding this, he says I am the beginning of the creation of God, indicating he knew God's original plan. The writings of the apostle John are not the plans of his father for his bride Laodicea. They are a clear revelation of what Satan would do to the church. He could see how his bride had gotten wrapped up in Satan's plans. He is the beginning of the creation God indicates; he is the way out.

At this point, there is no hostility toward his bride. He simply says, "I counsel you to buy of me gold tried in the fire." This is another prime example of oversight and control. He is outside of the situation not by choice. Instead of getting in rivalry, he takes the lead and gives the correct counsel for his bride to come out. A prime example of this is in Luke 10:38–42. Jesus enters into a small village to Martha's house. Her sister Mary is there also. Since it is Martha's house, she feels the need to extend hospitality to her guests. While she is working, Mary is there sitting and learning at the feet of Jesus. Martha has gotten wound up because she is doing all the work. When she has the opportunity to speak to Jesus, she tries to pull him down into the array of feelings she has going on. She tried to pull him into her atmosphere by saying don't you care that I'm doing all the work and Mary is just sitting there. He exercises oversight and doesn't allow Martha to pull him into her poisoned atmosphere. Then he gives clear direction. He says, "Martha you are cumbered with much care," indicating his awareness of her feeling base. He also says, "Mary has chosen the good part, and I will not take it away from her." It seems as if he left Martha lost in her world of emotion. But really, he gave her a way out, and that is to hear the word of God.

The element of human nature causes men to get tangled up and off track at times. The godly man must have the ability to see his original purpose and return to it, for therein lay salvation for his family and himself.

Lesson 21

- Jesus is the end of all things, therefore, he is the answer to all life's problems.
- Godly men must know how to stay out of rivalry with their wives and give oversight based on the word of God.
- Godly men and women put themselves under authority.

Transparency

Jesus says he is the one that lives but was dead. In order for Jesus to save his bride, he had to die. He died but yet lives. This is the process of salvation for his bride, dying to live. In the time that we live, there is much talk about transparency. Whereas transparency in finances of ministry is crucial, personal transparency to men can be devastating. In one aspect, transparency is an enemy to men. Because of the way they are designed, self-exposure is self-brutality. For this cause, the attitude of being closed up has been attributed to men. Without the correct environment that safely handles the inner softness of his manhood, he cannot open up. If he does, he opens himself up to abuse. This aspect of transparency is an enemy of manhood. It is because of this attitude that many men are dying inside. The secrets they are holding are cancerous and slowly destroying the vitality of their manhood.

In another aspect, transparency is exactly what men need to be healed. The godly man realizes that if he doesn't deal with his inner issues, he will drift through life without an anchor. It affects his relationships, work, and life in general. The characteristic of dying such that you might live is critical to his survival. With transparency being such a condemning issue for men, yet necessary, how can it be accomplished?

First of all, he must have the right environment to become transparent. This environment is defined out of a healthy relationship between mother and son. If a man wants to know what his correct environment for transparency is, he should study his relationship with his mother. A healthy mother/son relationship provides a place of rest and a nonthreatening atmosphere. Here he can share the thoughts of his heart without worry of being abused. It moves from there to his wife. If she is a woman of understanding, he can find a place of transparency there. Unfortunately, for a lot of men, they have had neither. Therefore, he must find the right leader, friend, men's group, and wife who understands the delicateness of his manhood. They will provide a safe environment where he can expose himself. The exposition of his faults brings healing in his life. When a man exposes himself, it is a death. For a godly man to die is to live. Therefore, the health of manhood depends upon the exposition of his faults in the proper environment. Manhood health is also the proper handling of manhood in the right environment.

Lesson 22

- The secret pain that men hold is detrimental to man's health. They have to be dealt with in the right environment.

Fitting the Pattern

God is the architect of the universe. As mentioned above, there are design patterns all around us. Once we find the pattern of a thing, we can operate in it. One pattern is gravity: what goes up must come down. Another pattern is the sand that sets the bounds for the oceans to never completely overtake the land. Even with people, there are patterns. If you fit them to pattern, they will work also.

There is a pattern for men, women, and children. Because we are freewill agents, there is great variation in humans, yet there is a basic pattern that when adhered to will work.

The first step in seeing the pattern of people work as designed is transformation into a godly men and women. This development is crucial in people patterns. The first people pattern I want to deal with is children. John saw Jesus as being one with the voice of many waters. It represents the authority for discipline and correction in his voice alone. Children that are being raised after God's pattern and in the presence of their father understand the stern voice. The pattern for raising godly children is really simple and hinge on two basic principles: correction and direction. The Bible says, "Who the Lord loves, he chastens and none of his children are without chastisement." Chastising is simply correcting. Children are wired by God to love the one that corrects them. In God's pattern, love and correction are equal terms.

The second thing that is vitally important for raising godly children is direction. Children are in the hands of a mighty one as arrows. When pointed in the proper direction, they will contend with the enemy and build the kingdom of God. That enemy is Satan.

The next people pattern is men. Men are really simple beings. The key to them is understanding their tenderness and handling it the right way. There is one thing that a man knows how to do well, and that is to be a son. He learns it from his father and mother. Tempered within is the tender caring of a mother along with the toughness of a father. Therefore, the secret to a man is handling him like a son without violating him as a man.

For this cause, a man shall leave the provision of his father and become a provider, and the tenderness of his mother to be entrusted to the tenderness of his wife.

A simple example of how to handle men would be this. In a household, there is a father, mother, and a child. Mother is frying chicken for dinner. The child comes in, wanting a piece of chicken. Mother says, "Wait till I finish cooking." Father comes in after the same manner and picks a drumstick and begins to eat. The action of the child and the husband are so similar, they could be easily classified the same. The actions of the woman affirms the man and classifies the child. If he is the head of the house and provider, then there should be no response to eating the drumstick. That is the response of a wife to her husband. If she says,

"Put it back and wait", she acts as mother and classifies him as one of her children. In doing so, she violates the fragile shell of manhood's spiritual and family authority. Manhood resembles childhood so closely; be careful to handle it correctly. It is the loaf of bread or the carton of eggs in the groceries. Always bag it separately.

It is unfortunate that the treatment of a mother toward her son is based upon her actually carrying him inside. Imagine the nurturing and care that will be given to that child. Before the child is born, she as a wife should have already given it to her husband. For this cause shall a man leave his mother and cleave to his wife.

The final people pattern is that of women. I am not a woman, so this is a single man's attempt to describe one of God's most complex creatures. Man was made out of simple dirt, but woman was made from a rib with DNA, flesh, bone, blood vessels, and veins. Compared to dirt, that translates complex. Women are complex creations of God.

There are several concepts that pattern women. The premise is not what she does but what the godly man does. Part of making a woman work in her pattern is what the man does. First of all, he must show exclusive commitment. She has to be secure in the fact that she has no threat to her relationship from without—by other women—or from within—abandonment by her husband. This allows the full spectrum of womanhood to come into display. Within it is the part that has to be controlled by the husband, and that is desire. Her desire shall be to her husband; he will control it. Controlling is simply aligning it with the word of God or the voice of wisdom especially when overwhelmed.

Another pattern of woman is tied into desire, and that is feeling. Momentary feeling is not her destiny. Despite how real her feelings may be at the moment, it is not what she ultimately wants. Because the husband has violated her trust, she may feel at the moment that she wants a divorce. What she really wants is exclusive relationship with her husband, along with their children. If he acts on the feeling, they may get divorced. If he meets the need of her pattern, they will have a strong family.

God designed women to be givers of life. When she is pregnant, she can feel what is growing inside. Men can only imagine, but what's inside is real. Not only is she a giver of life physically but in every aspect of life. You must be careful what you plant into her because what's inside will feel real. This is why it is predicated upon the man to give her the right atmosphere. The actions of the man causes something to grow inside her whether constructive or destructive; it is real to her at the moment. By using the characteristics of a godly man, at least two things will happen. First of all, she will *feel* safe. She will *feel* secure. She will *feel* protected. She will *feel* loved. Her feelings are anchored. Secondly, she will build a safety net for her husband on to her children.

If she is mishandled, she doesn't *feel* safe. She doesn't *feel* secure. She doesn't *feel* protected. She doesn't *feel* loved. She has no anchor. There is an array of feelings going on inside her, and they are real. She is acting out of the array of those feelings, which many times can be very destructive. There are a lot of women in this condition because they have not had a father around them to make them feel safe. It is ever so prevalent in the African American community. This woman breeds anxiety, mental breakdown, depression, oppression, bipolar, and childhood disorders. They are growing inside, and they are real.

Conclusion

In conclusion, I want to reiterate marriage is the basic building block of society. When it is misunderstood and abandoned, havoc is wreaked in our communities. Societal manhood has let down womanhood. It is time to begin the healing process. Individually, there are men in place, and they provide for their families. These relationships are breeding healthy children. Thank God for them.

As stated earlier , 30 percent of children are born out of wedlock, and in the African American community, nearly 70 percent. These numbers alone say that manhood has mishandled womanhood. What is being birthed in society is not right, but it is real.

Jesus knows how to fix the mishandled church, and if we follow his pattern, womanhood can begin to heal also. He loved the church and gave himself for her.

Love in a woman comes by what you do for and to them. Better said, it is felt. Men are different; with them, love is a conscious decision. Even though what you do for him shows love, he has to decide to love. This is why giving a flower to a man is a nice gesture. The action and concern is noted, but it will not make him feel loved. He has to decide to love. Once he makes that decision, the array of things done for him shows love. The Bible teaches women to respect their husbands, but it commands men to love their wives.

In healing womanhood, I want to look at it from an individual perspective, then in the perspective of collective manhood and womanhood.

Jesus applied the fix to the church. He made a conscious decision to love. While we were yet sinners, Christ died for the ungodly. He was prepped for the onslaught of disorder that would come at him from the church. He knew the design and pattern. Therefore, he could fit it to the pattern, and it could work. Through his character, he cleaned the church. He made it healthy again such that he could have a relationship.

With the number of children being born out of wedlock, it becomes more and more likely that men will come in contact with a woman that is lost in an array of feeling. You cannot build a strong family with her. Is she a bad person? No, she is what ungodly men have made her, and she has to be unraveled. As individual men, we must put on the characteristic of a godly man. He is not in a game with women. He knows and understands who he is and who she is. He also knows where she is and has to go. His approach is focused and determined.

He is armed to die such that he, the wife, and family can live. His survival as a godly man depends upon having a committed relationship with a woman. Therefore, his focus is not to play, but to be committed. Proverbs 18:22 says, "Whoso findeth a wife findeth a good thing, and obtaineth favour with the Lord." He is looking for the right type of woman, one that can advance the plans of God in his life. She may or may not be saved, sanctified, and filled. If she is, great, and he can move forward, full speed ahead. Ideally, she should be saved, sanctified, and filled, but if not, he knows the condition and has the power to change it. If she is, it still does not dismiss the fact that she may be wrapped up in an array of feeling.

Just think of all the single women and single mothers at church. Since he knows his work is cut out, man may very well find a woman that doesn't meet church criteria but has solid family structure he can work with more easily. Jesus died for the church, cleaned it up, and presented it to himself. It is the characteristics of a godly man that cleans a woman and unwraps her from her array of feelings. This takes the toughness of manhood along with patience and the true vision of a healthy wife. He knows she did not get there overnight, and he doesn't have a magic wand. It's going to take some time. At the onslaught of her feelings, it may even take dying. The godly man knows not to get entangled in the array of feeling but takes the oversight and moves her to where she should be.

The individual man that I see is one of divine purpose. His interaction with a woman is based out of godly principles. The more individual men develop after the characteristics of a godly man, the more we will see womanhood at large begin to heal.

The concepts of cohabitation and friends with benefits are, either man traps, or, to coin a phrase, masculated female ideology. They both destroy God's design for marriage. The ungodly man has convinced a woman to live with him, bear children, and have all the benefits of marriage without the commitment. This is what I call a man trap. It is perfect for a man, and he can walk out from it any time he wants. It is degrading to a woman because she has been saying within, "He will eventually marry me."

The masculated female is the one that has taken charge of her life and doesn't need anything from a man but his person. The term *masculated* deals with a mishandled woman. When a man is not there to do what he is supposed to, the woman does what she has to. The process causes masculation. She calls the shots and can use men the same way that men have used women. She still loses because it is hard to use a man sexually unless he really loves her.

Womanhood at large is sick and is breeding an array of dysfunction. What is inside of it is real, but it is not right. Therefore, it is going to take manhood to fix the problems it has created by the mishandling of womanhood. When I think of manhood, I think in terms of the community at large or collective. For instance, in a family where there is a husband, no one comes into his home without giving an account, and children must also give account. If his child gets into some kind of trouble, he does not leave it to others to correct his child. He deals with it. So he is a guardian in his home and his family.

Manhood at large should be the same way. In the African American community, I've watched the police come in and take our children away in numbers. Why is it so? Manhood has not dealt with its children. It has been left up to someone else to correct them without vested interest. Our children are suffering because the arms of manhood are not saying, "Those are our boys, and we will deal with them."

In the absence of protective manhood, instability creeps in. Instability brings fear and mental problems. Because we live in a monetary-driven society, the problems of insufficient manhood is capitalized on by applying a diagnosis to the problem and prescribing a drug that is only a pain reliever and does not fix the problem.

I encourage men, Christian and non-Christian alike, to take the characteristics of a godly man for yourself, and one by one, let's join together to repair ourselves, wives, manhood, and womanhood.

Printed in the USA
CPSIA information can be obtained
at www.ICGtesting.com
CBHW071545110424
6730CB00004B/14